How to win at
Poker
and
Bridge

This book is abridged from:

Beginner's Guide to Limit Hold'em, first published by D&B Publishing
P.O. Box 18, Hassocks, West Sussex, BN6 9WR, UK
www.dandbpublishing.com
ISBN: 9781904468219
Copyright © 2007 in text: Byron Jacobs
Copyright © 2007 in artworks: D&B Publishing
Copyright © 2007 D&B Publishing

and

Concise Bridge first published by: D&B Publishing
P.O. Box 18, Hassocks, West Sussex, BN6 9WR, UK
www.dandbpublishing.com
ISBN: 9781904468141
Copyright © 2007 in text: Sally Brock
Copyright © 2007 in artworks: D&B Publishing
Copyright © 2007 D&B Publishing

Note: The author and publishers have made every effort to ensure that the information given in this book is accurate, but they cannot accept liability for any resulting loss or damage to either property or person, whether direct or consequential and howsoever rising.

Welcome to *The Independent* guide to how to win at poker and bridge. Poker and bridge are, for different reasons, widely regarded as the greatest card games. Poker is the classic game of awareness, psychology and nerve, while bridge rewards the skills of logic and deduction. In this book, and in two of the glossy booklets that follow next week in *The Independent*, we will be examining these games and revealing how the best players plan and execute their strategies.

Nowadays, thanks to the internet, poker is everywhere. There are literally hundreds of online sites, numerous TV programmes and even entire channels devoted to the game. The top players can win millions in prize money but the great thing about poker is that anyone – literally anyone – can win a big tournament. In 2003, the aptly-named Chris Moneymaker won the World Series of Poker and bagged a cheque for $2.5m. He had obtained his seat by virtue of winning a $40 online qualifier and this was his very first "live" event. Only in poker could an enthusiastic amateur hope to win a world championship.

This book will give you a good grounding in the basics of poker. There are many variants but this book will focus on the game of limit hold'em, which is the best game to grasp the fundamentals of poker. In the subsequent booklets we will be looking at more of the general principles of play and will be drawing on examples from no-limit hold'em, which is the form of poker mainly used for tournament play. It will also demonstrate how the best players think at the table and reveal some of their key strategies.

The popularity of bridge was probably at its height in the 1930s when the American showman Ely Culbertson promoted it, first in the US and later worldwide. Famously, he played in a match against a British team over a number of days in the window of Selfridges. These days the game is having to withstand tough competition in terms of popularity from the vast range of games available on the internet. However, it has a lot going for it that internet games do not: in particular, it is an extremely sociable activity.

This book assumes little in the way of card-playing skills, and takes you through the basics of the game. Next week, in the booklet, you will be introduced to different techniques. If this most fascinating of games is beginning to take hold of you by then, your next step should be to enrol on a course of lessons at one of the many local bridge clubs around the country. If nothing else, it is a great way to make friends.

Contents

Poker

Bridge

Poker

by Byron Jacobs

Chapter 1

Why play poker?

The online poker revolution

Poker has witnessed an explosion of interest in recent years. The arrival of online cardrooms on the internet means that there are now thousands of cash games and tournaments available 24 hours a day at hundreds of different sites. The incredible interest that these sites generate can be seen from the valuation of nearly $5 billion which was attached to the leading online site, PartyPoker.com, when it floated in mid-2005.

The internet has made poker far, far more accessible than it ever was. The easy availability of online games means that anyone can play at any time. It is no longer necessary to seek out a cardroom in your local area, find your way over there and then possibly wait around until a free place becomes available. If you have a computer with an internet connection you can download software, register with a site and be playing poker within five minutes. And this is only to play your first game. Once you have installed the software and are registered then the next time you want to play you can be enjoying live action within 15 seconds.

Everyone is playing poker. I have played in online games with doctors, lawyers, social workers, midwives, housewives, students, celebrities, professional players, world champions and even one major Hollywood star. As with everything internet-related, online poker has integrated the world into a global village beyond anything that could have been anticipated by Marshall McLuhan.

A couple of years ago I was playing in a five-handed game. When you play online you use an alias (a handle) to identify yourself, but also give the area that you come from. Obviously players can lie about this but there seems no great incentive to do so. At the time I was residing in Hove in Sussex. My four opponents hailed from: Melbourne in Australia; San Francisco in the USA; Vancouver in Canada; and finally from Brunswick Square, which is approximately 150 yards from where I was living.

Serious money

The world championship of the poker world is the World Series, which is held every summer in Las Vegas. In this event, players "buy-in" with $10,000 and the accumulation of these entry fees makes up the prize pool. When a player loses their chips they are eliminated and play continues until one player has all the money. Prizes are typically paid out to the top 10 per cent on a sliding scale with the winner receiving the lion's share.

In 2001, this event had 613 entries and the eventual winner, Juan Carlos Mortensen of Madrid, took home $1.5 million. The runner-up won just over $1 million. This was fairly typical of this tournament at the time. However, with the advent of online play it is now possible to enter qualifiers (known as satellites) and, by winning such an event, a player gets a prize of a "free" buy-in to the World Series. These events have proved to be enormously popular and, as a consequence, entries for the World Series have increased dramatically.

In 2003, there were 839 entries and the eventual winner was the wonderfully-named Chris Moneymaker of the US, who took home $2.5 million. The remarkable feature of his achievement was that this was the very first "live" tournament he had played, and that he obtained his seat by winning a $40 qualifier on the internet!

By 2004 things had really taken off and at the start of play there were an astonishing 2,576 competitors – three times the number from the previous year. The winner was Greg Raymer of the US, who scooped $5 million for his victory. He too was an internet qualifier. Even the player finishing in fifth place took home more than $1 million, and number 27 in the final lists won $120,000.

The 2005 event saw 5,661 entrants for the World Series with total prize money at nearly $53 million. This is, by far, the biggest ever prize fund for a sporting event. The winner, Joseph Hachem, walked away with $7.5 million, with the runner-up, Steve Dannenmann, netting $4.5 million. Everyone who made it through to the last day's play and final table (nine players) pocketed a minimum of $1 million. Presumably it will not be long before the total prize money in this event tops $100 million.

Hold'em poker

There are many different ways to play poker. Those of you who have not played for many years are probably familiar with the classic variants such as draw poker and seven-card stud. However, over the past two decades hold'em has become firmly established as the most popular form of poker. It is the most popular poker game played in casinos and it is also the most popular game played online. In this book I am going to give you a thorough grounding in the game of limit hold'em.

How does hold'em work?

Hold'em employs the concept of "community cards" – cards which are shared by all players at the table. Every player is dealt two cards which comprise their hand, and then five cards are dealt face up in the centre of the table. These are the so-called community cards and are also known as the board. The aim of the game is to combine your two cards with the five board cards to make the best possible poker hand.

To this end you are allowed to use either one or both of your hole cards. If, at the end of play, your hand is better than those of your opponents, then you get to win the pot. The other way to win a pot is to have all of your opponents fold (ie throw away their hands) before the showdown. Then you win regardless of your cards. It is permissible, but unlikely, that you would want to use neither of your hole cards. In that case you would be playing the board and nobody else could possibly have a weaker hand.

Why play limit hold'em?

As we already know, hold'em is the most popular form of poker. If you want to get involved in the poker explosion then you will have to know how to play hold'em. The game played in all the major tournaments and, indeed, in the World Series is hold'em. Secondly, it is easier to learn than the other poker variants. The other most popular poker variant is Omaha and this game is, in a sense, a more complex version of hold'em.

What does 'limit' mean?

"Limit" refers to the betting structure. There are three ways in which hold'em (and indeed all other poker games) can be played: no-limit, pot-limit and fixed limit (usually known simply as "limit"). In no-limit, you are entitled to bet any amount of money at any time – the only caveat being that you must actually have that money on the table in front of you at the time. Suddenly delving into your wallet when you hit a big hand is, unsurprisingly, not allowed. Pot-limit allows you to bet any amount of money up to the current value of the pot. In limit your bet is a fixed unit which is defined by the level of the game. This makes limit hold'em a simpler game (to learn at least) than pot- or no-limit. In these games, big bets can suddenly appear out of nowhere and the size of the pot can escalate alarmingly. This does not happen in limit. The pots can get big – and they frequently do – but this happens gradually and not as the result of one huge bet. Limit hold'em is a better game for beginners than the other variants. If you make a mistake in pot- and no-limit you are vulnerable to losing your entire stack on a single hand. If you make a mistake in limit play you will dribble away some money but a single hand will not wipe you out.

Betting limits

Limit hold'em can be played at a wide variety of levels and online sites offer games ranging from those played for tiny amounts of money to those played for quite considerable sums. The level of the game is defined by two monetary amounts, the first being the small bet and the second being the big bet. The big bet is always precisely twice the size of the small bet. Thus typical games are $0.50-$1 limit hold'em, $2-$4 limit hold'em; $10-$20 limit hold'em; $40-$80 limit hold'em; and even $1,000-$2,000 limit hold'em. In his book, *The Professor, The Banker and the Suicide King*, Michael Craig catalogues private hold'em games that were played at limits of up to $100,000-$200,000.

I would, naturally, recommend that, as a beginning player, you start to play at a level where you are very comfortable with the potential losses. However, throughout this book I shall give examples of play from various different limits.

Show me the money

Poker is all about money. Although social games are occasionally played for buttons, matchsticks, milk bottle tops or whatever, at the end of the day poker doesn't make much sense if you are not playing for money. All online sites offer play-money games where you can try out the games playing purely for the fun of it. However, I would recommend that you only spend a small amount of time playing these games and only do this to familiarise yourself with the workings of the site and the game. The problem with playing when there is no money at stake is that there is no incentive (either for you or for your opponents) to try and play properly. It is crucial to develop a "feel" for hold'em (there will be much more on this later) and this is impossible in such artificial situations.

I would strongly recommend that – once you are comfortable with your understanding of the game – you begin playing as soon as possible in cash games, even if they are for very small amounts. All sites spread a $0.50-$1 limit hold'em game and numerous sites offer micro-limit games, playing for sums such as $0.10-$0.20. A reasonable rule of thumb is that you need to sit down at a table with a stack which is approximately 25 times the big bet. Thus, to sit in a $5-$10 game you need about $250. However, you can play at the $0.50-$1 limit with just $25. If this is more than you want to risk, then a micro-limit game of $0.10-$0.20 would require a stack of just $5. Players who play cash games – regardless of how high or low the level – usually take them seriously. You need to be able to play your poker in a serious frame of mind against other serious players, and you won't get this experience from play-money games.

Developing a feel

My emphasis throughout this book will be emphatically to try and give you a feel for how to play the game of limit hold'em. When learning the game myself, I read a number of books and absorbed advice such as to call from the button with a pair of fives only if three or more players had already called before me. This I dutifully did – the only problem being I had no idea why. I did not have a feel for what I was trying to achieve with this pair of fives, other than that it would be nice if another one popped up on the flop.

Here is another example. I would learn that when I was first to bet in the pot I should fold with A-10, but I should open with a raise when holding A-J, unless the game was very tight, in which case I should probably fold A-J too. However, if my A-J was suited, then I could play the hand. Really? How fascinating. What terrible calamity would befall me if I played this A-J offsuit in a tight game? Perhaps my computer would explode, or maybe someone would call the police.

And, come to that, what is a tight game anyway? I certainly had no idea, and I firmly believe that such advice is more or less useless for beginning players.

A further reason to try and develop a feel is that online limit poker is played pretty fast. You usually have a maximum of 15-20 seconds to make your decisions. This may seem frighteningly fast right now, but once you get involved in the play you will see that many decisions are more or less automatic. You will find that 90 per cent of plays at the table are made within a couple of seconds. If you use most of your time allowance for each decision you will soon irritate the other players at the table. These players often have the attention span of a gnat, and cannot bear to go more than five seconds without getting their "buzz" from the action. If you deprive them of this they will be quick to let you know in the chat box.

Chapter 2

Introducing the board

Using seven cards

A hold'em hand is – at the end of the deal – the best five-card hand you can make from the combination of your own two cards and the five cards on the board. There are 21 possible ways you can combine your two cards with the five board cards to make a hand, and before you can go any further you must become adept at being able to recognise, at a glance, what your hand is.

You can use both of your cards, just one of them or – unusually – purely the cards on the table. In this final case you are said to be playing the board and this is a rather sad situation to be in as nobody else can possibly have a worse hand than you.

The main things to look for in the seven-card combinations are:

1) Cards of the same rank

These cards will make pairs or trips (another way to describe three of a kind) and lead to hands such as two pair, three of a kind or even a full house.

2) Suitedness

If five of your collection are suited, then you have a flush.

3) Connectedness

If five of your collection run in sequence, then you have a straight.

Take a look at the following combinations:

Example 1

The Board

Your Hand

Here your king and jack of hearts combine with the three high hearts on the board to make a royal flush – a fantastic hand.

Example 2

The Board

Your Hand

Your jack and ten of hearts combine with the three hearts on the board to make a straight flush – another wonderful hand.

Example 3

The Board

Your Hand

You hold two threes and they match up with the two threes on the board to make four of a kind – yet another major hand.

> **NOTE: When you have a two cards of the same rank in your hand, you hold a "pocket pair". In this example you have pocket threes.**

Example 4

The Board

Your Hand

You have a pair of nines (pocket nines) and this is matched by the nine on the board. Combining this three of a kind with the pair of eights on the board generates a full house.

Example 5

The Board

Your Hand

You have a flush. You have two hearts in your hand and there are three on the board.

Example 6

The Board

Your Hand

You have only the A♣, but the four clubs on the board generate your flush. The Q♠ is irrelevant. You hold the best possible missing club, so even if another player has a flush, you have the best one!

Example 7

The Board

Your Hand

Your J-8 weaves in with the 10-9-7 to form a straight with the sequence J-10-9-8-7.

Example 8

The Board

Your Hand

Again you have a straight. The sequence A-Q-J-10 is on the board, and you can use either of your kings to plug the gap and make a broadway straight. As with Example 6 you will use only one of your cards and, in this particular case, which one you actually use is irrelevant.

Example 9

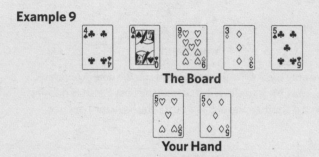

The Board

Your Hand

You have a pair of fives and there is a third five on the board. This gives you three of a kind.

Example 10

The Board

Your Hand

Here is another way to make three of a kind. This time there is a pair of queens on the board and you have a queen in your hand. Note that in this case you are also using your nine to make your hand because your complete hand is Q-Q-Q-K-9 (your nine outranks the eight and six on the board). This could prove to be important if another player also has a queen in their hand.

NOTE: When you make a three of a kind hand by using one of your cards to match a pair on the board you have trips. Thus, in the above example, you have trip queens. If you have a pair in your hand and this is matched by a card on the board you have a set. Thus in Example 9, you hold a set of fives.

Example 11

The Board

Your Hand

This example is similar to the previous one, only now your 5 ♥ "doesn't play". Your hand is trip aces – A-A-A-J-7 – you cannot do better than use the board cards for your sidecards. If another player also has an ace in their hand they will beat you if their other card is higher than a seven (or if they have a seven or four which will generate a full house).

Example 12

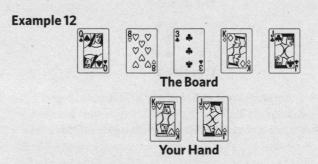

The Board

Your Hand

Here you have two pair. Your king and jack have both found partners on the board. You have two pairs, kings up.

Example 13

The Board

Your Hand

Here you have just one pair – aces. However, you have a very good side-card with the queen. If another player has a one pair hand you will only lose to them if they hold precisely A-K. Although this is "only" a one-pair hand, it is an absolute bread and butter hand at hold'em. I would guess that more hands are won at hold'em by a single pair of aces than by any other holding.

Example 14

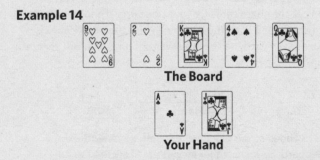

The Board

Your Hand

You haven't made anything at all and are stuck with ace high. Nevertheless, it's not a bad ace high – in fact it is the best possible, A-K-Q-J-9. It is not that unusual to win a hold'em hand with just a high card.

Example 15

The Board

Your Hand

You have a two-pair hand – tens and twos. However, everybody else in the hand will also have a two-pair hand if they hold a queen, a nine or a seven (or even a pocket pair). You will have to hope that your opponents are holding either a nine or a seven (making two-pair hands which lose to yours) rather than a queen (making two-pair hands which beat yours).

Example 16

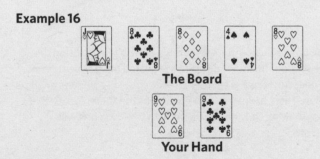

The Board

Your Hand

You have a full house. Your pair of nines combines with the three eights on the board. However, other players are likely to have full houses too. Anyone with a jack in their hand or a higher pocket pair than your nines will make a bigger full house. However, you will beat a player who holds a four. Anyone with the missing eight will be putting on their best poker face.

Understanding hand strength

If you've looked carefully through the preceding material you should now understand that hands in hold'em are relative. If your poker background comes from social games of draw poker or seven-card stud, then it may be difficult to get a handle on this. In draw poker and seven-card stud hands such as flushes and full houses are very strong holdings. In hold'em there are shared board cards and so the value of holdings is relative. We can see this from the following examples:

Example 1a

Here you have a flush. Your 4♣ combines with four clubs on the board to make your flush. So, do you have a good hand? Well it's not bad but it does not take a great deal to beat you – all someone needs is a higher club. There are plenty of higher clubs out there: 5, 6, 8, 10, J, Q, K – seven in total. Only an opponent with the lowly 3♣ will be paying you off.

Example 1b

Here you again have a flush. Your K♣-J♣ combines with three clubs on the board to make your flush. How strong is your hand now?

Very strong. The only way that someone can beat you is if they hold precisely A-x in clubs and, while not impossible, this is not very likely. An opponent with just the bare A♣ has not completed a flush.

Example 2a

 Here you have a full house. Your pocket fours combine with the three nines on board to make a full house. A full house is a very big hand. So, how are you doing here? Badly is the answer. It is, again, just too easy for someone to have a better hand. Anyone with a jack or a king has a bigger full house. Anyone with the missing nine (also known as the "case" nine) swamps you with quad nines. Even a player with their own pocket pair will beat you if their pair is higher than your fours.

Example 2b

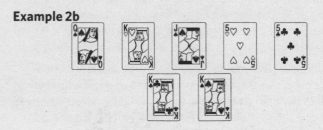

 Here you again have a full house. You have a set of kings and this has combined with the pair of fives on the board to make kings full of fives. This hand – as you might anticipate – is very strong. It is very difficult indeed for someone to have a better hand than you. In fact there is only one way this can happen – if they hold 5-5 for quad fives. This is highly unlikely.

Example 3a

Here you have a two-pair hand: kings and jacks. This is a very modest hand compared with the flush and full house that you held in Examples 1a and 2a. This hand, although much lower in ranking than either of those two, is actually very much stronger. There are no flush or straight possibilities and you hold the best possible two-pair hand. For someone to beat you they will need to have a set, with a pocket pair matching one of the board cards. Such holdings are quite rare.

Example 3b

Here you again have your two-pair hand: kings and jacks. In the previous example we discerned that this was a very powerful holding, so how does this one rate? The answer is very badly indeed – the hand is almost completely useless. There are four hearts on the board as well as the sequence K-Q-J-10. This means that anyone with an ace or a nine beats you with a straight, and anyone with a heart is beating you with a flush. It is highly unlikely that your hand is good.

The key point here is the "texture" of the board. In Example 3a the board was completely uncoordinated. The board in 3b is a different story entirely.

> *TIP: When assessing the strength of your holding, a key feature is the texture of the board. Moderate holdings such as one or two pair are greatly weakened if the board is coordinated (allowing straight possibilities) or predominantly of one suit (allowing flush possibilities).*

Example 4a

Here you have a moderate hand – just a pair of kings with a queen kicker. Nevertheless, this is a pretty good holding. You have top pair with the second best possible kicker, and the board is not coordinated at all. With a small number of opponents, it is probable that you have the best hand. The most likely way that you are beaten here is if an opponent has A-K. However, there are a number of plausible holdings for your opponents where you are winning, e.g. K-J, K-10, A-9, 10-9 plus all pocket pairs (barring aces) that have not received help on the board. In all cases your opponent will have a weaker one-pair hand.

Example 4b

Here again you have your pair of kings. In fact you actually have a two-pair hand – kings and tens – but since the 10-10 is on the board and is shared by everybody, the value of your hand is with the pair of kings. This holding is very much weaker than the one from Example 4a. Here there are two major problems and one small one.

The first major problem is the ace on the board. This means that anyone with just an ace has aces up, beating your kings up. The second big problem is the pair of tens on the board. Anyone with a ten has (at the least) trip tens and this also beats you. A smaller, but nevertheless important, concern is that although you have the best possible kicker with the queen, it doesn't play and your hand is kings and tens with an ace kicker (K-K-10-10-A). This means that anyone else with a king will (at worst) tie with you. Even if they hold K-2, their hand will still be the same as yours.

From these examples, we can note that there are some key features which help to discern whether a holding is strong or weak:

1) Using both cards

It is generally much better if both of your cards are working for you. Whether this is to make a straight, a flush, two pair or even to provide a good kicker, your hand is likely to be much stronger when both cards play.

2) An opponent needs to use both cards to beat you

This is a straightforward corollary to the first point. If an opponent can better you with just a single card (as in Examples 1a, 2a, 3b and 4b) then this is a weakness of your hand. If they must have both cards working for them to beat you (as in Examples 1b, 2b, 3a and 4a) then this strengthens your hand.

3) Coordinating with the higher/highest cards on the board

A hand that links in with the higher cards on the board is stronger than one that links in with the lower cards. This is seen clearly in Examples 4a and 4b.

The nuts

The nuts is a frequently-used poker term. It simply means the best possible hand with the given board cards. It is not always the most likely hand, sometimes it is rather improbable. However, it is useful to be able to recognise what the nut holding is. Here are some examples.

Example 1

The nut hand is held by anyone with Q-J, generating the top straight.

Example 2

Now with three spades on board the nut hand will be a flush. Thus a player with K-x in spades holds the nuts. Anyone with Q-x in spades holds the "second nuts".

Example 3

The pair of tens changes everything again as now full houses become possible. The nut hand, however, is quad tens which will be held by anyone lucky enough to have the missing tens. Another very powerful holding is A-A, making the "nut full house" (ie other players can hold weaker full houses). This is the second nut hand and would be good enough to win over 99 per cent of the time.

Example 4

At first glance it looks as though there are no straights or flushes available, and so the best hand will be A-A for a set of aces. However, this is actually the second nut hand as 2-4 makes "the wheel" – the lowest possible straight (5-4-3-2-A).

Summary

The following should be borne in mind when you are "reading the board":

There is a pair on board

Full houses are possible. Someone could have four of a kind, but this is unusual.

There are no pairs but the board features three or more cards of the same suit

The best possible hand is a flush. There is an exception – if the flush cards are coordinated then a straight flush becomes possible.

There are no pairs and no flush possibilities

If there are three cards sufficiently close together in rank then a straight is possible. Otherwise a set is the best possible hand.

Chapter 3

The basics of play

How limit hold'em is played

Limit hold'em can be played with any number of players between two (heads-up) or 10 (a full ring game). Most games are played with between eight and 10 players at the table. Many players like to play short-handed games (typically featuring between four and six players) but this requires rather specialised skills and is not recommended for beginners. Other players like to play heads-up with just two players at the table. Such encounters can be great fun (and also profitable for a skilled player) but their dynamics are so different from full ring play that they almost constitute a completely different game. For the purposes of this introductory material I am going to discuss how play operates in a full ring game.

The players sitting at various positions around the table can be identified by their positions. These terms are in very common usage in poker literature and it is good to get used to them as soon as possible. Here is a table featuring ten players:

Table positions

The first player is Alan and he has a "button" in front of him to signify that he is, in principle, the dealer. In live play such as in a casino, the dealer would actually have a small round object, the button, placed in front of him, to signify his status. In online play this is represented graphically by a small on-screen blob. Alan will remain the dealer throughout the hand, regardless of whether he is still in the pot or not.

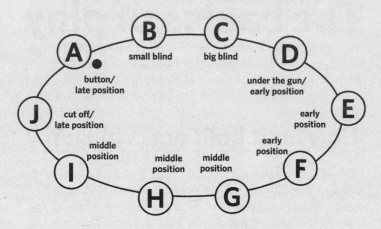

The next player to consider is the one to the button's immediate left. This position is the small blind and in our example here this spot is occupied by Belinda. Next comes Charlie who finds himself in the spot known as the big blind.

To the immediate left of the big blind is the position known as the under the gun (UTG). In our table above this position is held by Donna. Donna, along with Edward and Fiona who are to her immediate left, are known as early position players.

The next three players, Gary, Heather and Ian are all middle position players. The player sitting to Ian's immediate left is Julie, who is in the cut-off seat. Julie and Alan, who is the dealer, are collectively known as late position players.

The position of the button rotates clockwise around the table. Thus on this hand Alan has the button but on the next deal it will move to Belinda when Charlie and Donna will find themselves in the small and big blinds respectively. After Belinda, it will be Charlie's turn to deal and so on.

The blinds

There has to be something in the pot at the start of play, otherwise there is nothing to fight for. In hold'em this is handled by having two blinds: a small blind and a big blind. These players are obligated to put money into the pot at the start of the hand. The small blind puts up a sum (typically) equivalent to half of a small bet and the big blind contributes a small bet. Thus in a $1-$2 game, the small blind is $0.50 and the big blind is $1, whilst in a $20-$40 game the sums are $10 and $20 respectively.

At some limits there is no simple way to halve the small blind. This is how three of these limits are usually dealt with:

Game	Small Blind
$3-$6 game	$1
$5-$10 game	$2
$15-$30 game	$10

Note the slight illogicality in that in the $3-$6 game the small blind is one-third of the big blind, whereasin the $15-$30 game it is two-thirds.

The play of the hand

After the blind money has been put in the pot each player is dealt two cards – their hand. There is now a round of betting known as the pre-flop betting round.

The unit for this betting round is a small bet. Thus in a $5-$10 game players will bet in units of $5. Players who like the look of their cards will be betting and raising, whilst players with unfavourable cards will be folding (also known as mucking). Players who fold their cards are out and will play no further part in the hand. We will discuss the betting at greater length very shortly.

The pre-flop betting round is unusual in that the first player to "speak" is the UTG. On all subsequent rounds the first player to speak will be the small blind. After the UTG player has acted, play moves clockwise around the table.

After the pre-flop betting is completed, three cards are dealt face up in the centre of the table. These three cards are known collectively as the flop and we now have the flop betting round. If the small blind is still in the pot (he may, of course, have folded during the pre-flop round of betting) then he will be the first to speak, followed by the big blind, the UTG and so on. The unit for the flop betting round is again one small bet.

Once the flop betting is completed, a single card is dealt to join the other three communal cards on the table. This card is known as the turn and after it has been dealt we have the turn betting. Again the small blind is first to speak. The unit for the turn betting round is one big bet – double the size of the pre-flop and flop rounds.

At the conclusion of the turn betting, a final card is dealt to join the other four in the middle. This is the river card and we now have the river betting. The unit for the river betting is again one big bet. All cards have now been dealt. When the river betting is complete players who are still in the pot show down their hands and the best hand takes the pot.

> **NOTE: There are four rounds of betting: pre-flop, flop, turn and river.**

Betting Round	Bet Size	In a $5-$10 game
Pre-flop	Big Blind	$5
Flop	Big Blind	$5
Turn	2 x Big Blind	$10
River	2 x Big Blind	$10

The betting

In limit hold'em the amount you can bet (or raise) at any point is fixed. A round of betting is completed when all players who are still active in the hand have contributed the same amount of money to the pot.

Responding to a bet

When the action comes to you and there has already been a bet – or a bet and one or more raises – then there are three options:

1) You can fold

Maybe you do not like the look of your hand or maybe you regard the amount of money that you need to put into the pot to stay active in the hand as too much. In that case, you can simply throw your hand away. You contribute no money to the pot and your participation in the hand is over.

2) You can call

Perhaps you have a middling hand. It might seem too good to throw away just yet, but maybe you are not sure where you stand. Now a good option is to call the bet. To do this you have to place an amount of money in the pot which matches the current level of the bet. Thus, if the current unit of the betting round is $5 and there has just been a bet (and maybe one or more calls), then you can call for $5. If there has already been a bet and a raise, then it will cost $10 to call.

3) You can raise

Maybe you like the look of your hand and suspect that you have the best chance to win the pot. Now you want to take the initiative and make the other players pay extra to stay with you – and so you raise. To do this you match the current bet and then add one extra betting unit for the raise. So, if there has just been a bet on a $5 round, then to raise you will put $10 into the pot. Now anyone who has only put $5 in so far will have to call your raise if they wish to continue.

Acting when there is no bet

Sometimes on a betting round it happens that when the action comes to you, no-one else has yet bet anything. Now you have two options:

1) You can check

You do not put any money into the pot but you remain in the hand.

Of course, someone may now bet subsequent to you and then you will be forced to (at least) call the bet if you wish to stay active in the pot. Sometimes, however, everybody checks and no money enters the pot on that particular betting round.

2) You can bet

You put the equivalent of one betting unit into the pot and oblige other players to (at least) call your bet if they wish to continue in the pot.

Note that it is not possible (for players not in the big blind) to check on the pre-flop betting round, as it is necessary to call the forced bet from the big blind. Thus no-one (excepting the big blind) can get to see the flop cards without committing some money to the pot.

Further notes on betting

1) Keeping the betting open

Whenever a player raises they are keeping the betting open. Every other player who is still in the pot will have to call the raise, and this will give them the opportunity to re-raise if they wish.

2) Closing the betting

At some point there will be only one player remaining who has not yet called the bet. If this player does call (rather than raising) then the betting is closed and play moves on to the next round. Note that if this player were to fold the effect would be the same – every player remaining in the pot would have called the bet and play would again move on to the next round.

3) Capping the betting

Raising and re-raising cannot go on indefinitely. In online games (this can vary slightly in live-action play) it is standard for the betting to be capped by the third raise. Thus if there is a bet, a raise and a re-raise then only one further raise is possible. The player making this final raise is said to be capping the pot. Thus on a $5 betting round the maximum that each player can contribute to the pot is $20 (a bet and three raises). If the action comes to you and the pot has already been capped, then you cannot raise. Your choices are limited to calling the bet or folding.

4) When everyone folds

If one player decides to bet or raise during the course of a betting round and everybody else folds, then the pot is immediately won by that player, regardless of their cards.

This may all sound terribly complicated, but it is actually quite straightforward and you will soon get the hang of it.

The Rake

You will not be surprised to learn that online poker sites make an awful lot of money, which is why they attract valuations of millions and even billions of dollars. The way they make their money is exactly the same as the way casinos and cardrooms make their money from poker – they take a rake out of each pot. The rake is the site's fee for managing the games and it is typically between $1 and $3 per pot, depending upon the final pot size. A typical rake might be as follows: $1 for a pot smaller than $30, $2 for a pot between $30 and $50 and $3 for a pot over $50. Sometimes the rake is capped at, say, $2 if the game has six players or less. Also, sites usually have a "no flop, no drop" policy meaning that if a hand is concluded pre-flop (with every player bar one folding) then no rake is deducted from the pot.

No-Limit Hold'em

The other way to play hold'em is to play no-limit. In no-limit hold'em a player can bet any amount of money at any time. This makes the game much more dangerous than limit as your entire stack is vulnerable any time you enter a pot. The structure of play though, is really the same as for limit hold'em with all the rules regarding checking, betting, raising and so on, still applying. However, you can bet any amount and you can raise any amount.

There is no compelling reason why hold'em should not be played at pot-limit, but it is quite rare. The limit and no-limit forms dominate.

Tournament Hold'em

The majority of major poker events (including the prestigious World Series of Poker) feature no-limit hold'em. In tournaments each competitor begins with the same amount of chips. The play is just as for a normal no-limit hold'em game, except that if you lose your stack you are eliminated from the event.

Play is speeded up by increasing the levels of the blinds at regular intervals. At the start of play the blinds may be a tiny fraction of the chip stacks, and players can survive by being conservative. However, towards the end of the event, the blinds have usually increased substantially and can represent significant percentages of players' stacks. When this happens (or when it becomes likely to happen) players can no longer be passive, or they will be blinded away.

Tournaments can vary enormously in the number of players competing. Small online tournaments are often played on just one table and are called sit'n'gos. They start with ten players and usually take less than an hour to complete. Larger events are played multi-table and, as players are eliminated, tables are merged to keep each table as full as possible. Small online events regularly start with 20 or 30 players while bigger ones might start with a few hundred. Such events can last for several hours. Major live tournaments such as the World Series of Poker often see starting line-ups of a thousand or more players and these events can run over several days.

Tournaments pay out the top places on a sliding scale. A sit'n'go featuring ten players with an entry fee of $10 (plus a little extra for the cardroom's registration fees) has $100 available in prize money. This is usually split with $50 to the winner, $30 to the runner-up and $20 to the player coming third. Bigger tournaments can provide huge prizes for the players making it down to the final three or four places.

Chapter 4

How hands develop

We have already practised the job of extracting our best five-card hand from the seven cards that are on the board after the final river card has been dealt. Now, however, we need to concentrate on how hands develop from the pre-flop stage through the flop, turn and river.

For the moment we will not worry about the betting – we are just going to see how hands can develop and specifically look at how worse hands can overtake better hands with helpful cards on the turn and/or river.

Before we examine closely how hands develop, I want to briefly introduce one other element of hold'em: the concept of outs.

The concept of outs

At any stage in a hand of hold'em, one player will have the best hand but the opposition will (almost always) have chances to improve significantly. The cards that help them to improve are called outs. Generally this is taken to mean cards that can improve your hand in such a way that your hand is now likely to overtake a previously better one.

Here is an example:

Andrew

Barry

Barry is playing a strong starting hand with the best possible non-pair hand, A-K. Andrew has a weaker holding with two lower cards. Barry is, of course, favourite, but all that can easily change as cards arrive on the board, and the values of the players' hands can alter dramatically.

Once the flop has been dealt, both sides find that they have a pair. Barry is currently ahead because his pair of kings beats Andrew's pair of nines. In order to improve and overtake Barry, Andrew will need to hit one of his outs. So, what are his outs?

Firstly notice that (for the moment at least) Andrew has no straight or flush possibilities. The only way he can overtake Barry is by improving to a two-pair or three of a kind hand.

The cards that will help him are nines (to generate three of a kind) or tens (to make two pair). The situation below shows a nine arriving on the turn:

Andrew now has three of a kind and is beating Barry. A ten will also do the trick:

Andrew now has two pair and is again beating Barry.

Thus, on the flop, Andrew has three tens and two nines which improve him to a winning hand. He has precisely five outs.

But what about if a seven appears on the turn? The situation is now as follows:

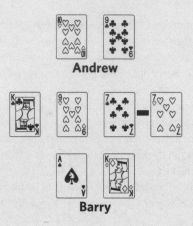

Andrew now has two pairs, nines and sevens, but he still hasn't overtaken Barry. The pair of sevens is on the board, so Barry can also use them to make a two-pair hand. His kings and sevens still beats Andrew's nines and sevens. The second pair is shared, so does not benefit either player (a player who happened to have a seven in his hand would benefit, of course).

This can continue on the river. If the river card is yet another seven we then have the following situation.

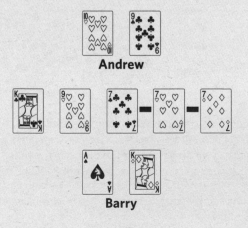

Andrew has improved yet again – he now has a full house, sevens over nines. The turn and river cards have improved his hand from one pair to two pair to a full house. Unfortunately, this improvement has all been in vain as Barry has improved in a similar way and now holds a full house sevens over kings and is winning.

This demonstrates two important principles in hold'em.

Better hands often remain better

Hands that are better on the flop often remain so all the way to the river, even though the hands improve in their rankings.

Holdings are relative

Having a high-ranking hand in hold'em is of limited use if it is very easy for other players to have high ranking hands too.

Hands with potential

It is quite common for cards to appear on the turn which do not immediately help either hand, but create further potential for improvement. Let's rewind back to the flop situation and imagine that the turn card is the 8♣. The situation is now as follows.

Andrew

Barry

This card has not improved either player's hand and Barry's pair of kings is still beating Andrew's pair of nines. However, it has given

Andrew tremendous potential for two reasons:

1) There are now three clubs on the board and he has a club in his hand. Any further club on the river will complete a flush for him.

2) He has a ten in his hand which, allied with the sequence 9-8-7 on the board creates the chance to make a straight. Any jack or six will complete this straight.

Previously Andrew had only five outs, but this turn card has hugely increased his potential to improve. How many outs does he now have? Let's count them, but in doing so we must be careful not to "double count" certain cards.

For a start, he has nine clubs for the flush. Secondly he has three jacks and three sixes for the straight (note that the J♣ and the 6♣ have already been accounted for with the flush draw – the first example of avoiding double counting). Finally has he two nines and two tens (careful not to include the 10♣). This makes a total of 9 + 3 + 3 + 2 + 2 = 19 outs! Quite an improvement from a mere five.

Tainted outs

However, it is important to note that Andrew cannot be certain how many of his outs are "good". For example if we change the hand slightly so that Barry holds the A♣ instead of the A♠ then we have the following situation.

Andrew

Barry

Now Andrew's outs with the clubs are useless. If a random club appears on the river, then he will have a king-high flush but Barry will complete an ace-high flush. In poker parlance, Andrew's club outs are tainted. The clubs are no longer good and his 19 outs are reduced to 10. Still, that is a better situation than the five he had on the flop.

In the real world

Obviously this is all theoretical as neither player knows what the other player holds. On the flop Andrew's pair of nines could – for all he knows – currently be the best hand. However, if his opponent bets the hand hard on the flop, he might assume that he is up against a pair of kings. In that case he has to decide whether he is justified in continuing in the pot, considering that he appears to be behind.

When the turn card comes, he really has no way at all to know whether his opponent has a club (or even two clubs) in his hand, and cannot know precisely how many outs he has – if indeed he has any. For example, if Barry has a hand such as A♣-Q♣, then he has already completed a flush, and Andrew has no outs whatsoever.

> **WARNING: Poker is a game of imperfect knowledge. Making judgments about where you stand in the hand and what your chances of improving are is an absolutely key skill in hold'em.**

Strong players who – inevitably – have a great deal of experience play-ing hold'em, recognise the patterns that appear and can make these assessments in an instant. They will know instinctively where they stand in the hand (for good or bad) and have a very good idea how likely they are to take down the pot. This is the skill that you must try to develop to become a consistently winning player.

Playing hands

In order to keep things simple there will be just two players battling it out. Of course, in actual real-life games (as in the practice hand we played through in Chapter 3) there may well be more players competing for the pot.

Example 1

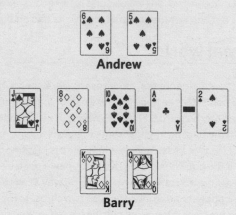

Andrew

Barry

Pre-flop

Andrew is playing speculatively with suited connectors, whereas Barry has a solid high-card combination which is suited.

Flop

On the flop Andrew had four cards towards a flush with his spade pair matching the two spades on the board. Andrew is thus on a flush draw and is hoping for another spade to complete his flush.

Barry could ally the J-10 combination on the board with his K-Q to create K-Q-J-10. This is four cards towards a straight and means he has a straight draw, needing an ace or a nine to complete his straight. Barry can complete his straight draw at either end, so his hand is an open-ended straight draw. A straight draw with only one possibility to complete it (eg 9-8-7-5 or A-K-Q-10) is known as a gutshot draw.

At this point neither side has a made hand, and Barry is currently winning with his king high beating Andrew's jack high. However, both hands have great potential to improve.

Turn

The turn card has done nothing for Andrew's prospects but it has completed Barry's straight (A♣-K♦-Q♦-J♠-10♠). Barry is now well ahead. However, Andrew has outs in the form of the missing spade cards. There are no complicating factors and so he has precisely nine outs.

River

It is Andrew's lucky day. He has made his flush on the river. Barry had the best hand but he has been outdrawn.

Example 2

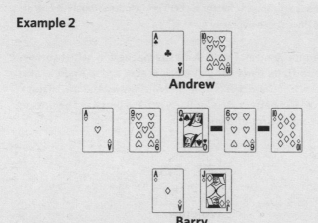

Andrew

Barry

Pre-flop

Both players have reasonable high cards. Barry is ahead because although they both have an ace, his jack is better than Andrew's ten. This means that Barry starts as a good favourite in the hand. Andrew will need to improve his holding by hitting a ten on the board (or making an unlikely flush or straight), as pairing his ace will be of no great help (Barry, obviously, will then also have a pair of aces). Barry is also helped by the fact that he has a suited combination.

Flop

On the flop both players have made a pair of aces. The ace is the highest ranking card on the flop, so we can say that both players have top pair. At the moment Barry is ahead because he has the better kicker, with his jack outranking Andrew's ten. If nothing much happens to change the structure of the board between now and the river, then Barry will take the pot thanks to his better kicker.

Turn

The turn card helps Andrew slightly. The six is a third heart, and means that Andrew has picked up a flush draw. Barry does not have any hearts in his hand and so the presence of a third heart on board is of no help to him, although – as discussed earlier – Andrew will not know this. The fact that it is a six also does nothing for Barry's hand. However, he is still ahead (better kicker) and Andrew must hit one of his outs on the river to overtake him.

River

Andrew gets lucky again. The 10 ♦ means that he now has a two-pair hand: aces and tens. Barry has only a pair of aces and so Andrew takes the pot. Barry's better kicker is no longer relevant as Andrew's hand has improved to a better category. Barry had the best hand before the river but he has been outdrawn again.

Example 3

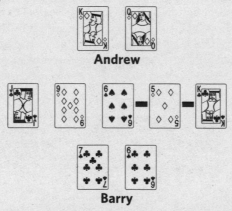

Andrew

Barry

Pre-flop

Here the players have similar holdings to those from Example 1, but the roles are reversed. Barry is speculating with suited connectors and Andrew has solid high cards which are also suited.

Flop

Here the flop has something for both players. Andrew has not made a pair but the sequence K-Q-J-9 gives him a gutshot draw which would be completed with a ten. His king and queen are also higher than any of the board cards and this means that they are overcards.

Overcards can be useful because they give you more chances to outdraw a stronger hand. Even if Barry has made top pair with, say J-10, then Andrew can still outdraw him by hitting a king or queen on the turn or river. Consider the situation if Andrew had 7♦-5♦ instead of his holding of K♦-Q♦. He would still have a gutshot draw (9-7-6-5, missing the eight) but no longer have any overcards. If Andrew then made a pair with either a five or seven coming on board, it would not help him if Barry happened to hold J-10. A pair of jacks would beat fives or sevens. Andrew's only chance would be to complete his gutshot or to receive very helpful cards on the turn and river resulting in an improbable flush or three of a kind. As it stands, Andrew's overcards give him many extra chances to improve to the winning hand. In this situation he has ten outs, these comprising three kings, three queens and four tens (completing the gutshot).

Barry has made bottom pair with a pair of sixes, but he is probably not thrilled about his hand. He can see that there are two higher cards on the board (J♣-9♦). If Andrew happens to have paired one of those cards, then Barry is struggling and will need to improve. However, as things stand, Barry is ahead with his pair of sixes.

Turn

The turn card is a second diamond and this means that Andrew now has a flush draw, although his actual hand is still only king high. The fact that the card is a five means that Barry has picked up a gutshot draw (9-7-6-5). However this is actually irrelevant. Barry is currently winning with his pair of sixes and if an eight does happen to come on the river he will have received a useless piece of luck. His pair is enough to win in any case. It will be particularly irritating for him if the 8♦ appears. He will make a straight but will lose to Andrew's flush.

River

Andrew gets lucky for a third time. For all his wonderful drawing opportunities to flushes and straights, he actually ends up winning with a rather mundane pair of kings. However, this does demonstrate the importance of overcards on the flop.

Example 4

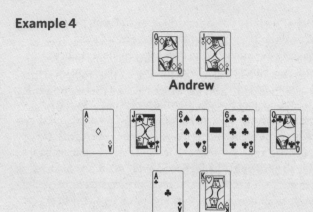

Andrew

Barry

Pre-flop
Both players have solid high cards. Andrew's are suited and connecting, so he has more chances to make straights and flushes, whereas Barry has the better high cards so he starts off in the lead.

Flop
Both players make a pair on the flop, but Barry is winning with his pair of aces, against Andrew's pair of jacks. In fact Barry has a strong hand here as his pair of aces is the best possible pair and his king is the best possible kicker. He is beating any hand that is not stronger than one pair. The flop, being of three different suits, is a rainbow flop, making eventual flushes improbable. Notice that there are no real drawing possibilities (to straights or flushes) for either player on the flop.

This flop situation is common with one player having a higher pair than another player. Here Andrew has five outs. He needs a jack or a queen to hit the board in order to improve his hand. The jack will make him a three of a kind, while a queen will make him two pairs. In both cases he will overtake Barry's one pair. Two possible jacks remain in the deck as well as three queens. So Andrew has five outs.

Turn
The turn card improves both player's hands from one-pair to two-pair hand. As this improvement is shared, it may seem irrelevant but it has an important effect and helps Barry's hand as we will now see.

River

Andrew gets a favourable river card yet again. This time however, it doesn't help him. Although his hand has improved from being two pair, jacks and sixes, to two pair, queens and jacks, the problem is that Barry has a bigger two pair – aces and sixes. Now we can see how the turn card subtly helped Barry's hand. It reduced Andrew's outs from five to two – only a jack on the river could help him.

Focusing on outs

We will now examine the concept of outs more carefully. All of the following situations occur after the flop and turn cards have been dealt and we will consider who is currently winning and how many outs the weaker hand has. At all times we must look carefully for the possibility of tainted outs.

Example 1

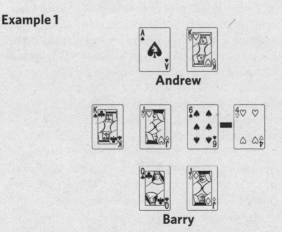

Andrew

Barry

Andrew is winning with a pair of kings against a pair of jacks. Barry has five outs: two jacks and three queens. This is the standard situation where you have a battle between pairs of different rank – the weaker side will usually be playing for five outs.

Example 2

Andrew

Barry

Andrew is winning. Both players have a pair of kings, but Andrew has the ace kicker. Barry has just three outs – the three missing nines for a two-pair hand. This situation is much worse for the weaker hand than the one in Example 1 – the problem being the shared king. Oddly, Barry's chances would be improved if he held a weaker hand! A hand such as J-10 or 6-5 he would offer five outs rather than just three.

Example 3

Andrew

Barry

Barry is winning with a pair of queens against a pair of eights. Andrew has 13 outs: four tens and four fives complete a straight, while three nines and two eights improve him to three of a kind and two pairs respectively.

> *NOTE: When the board becomes coordinated with straightening and flushing cards, then it becomes likely that weaker hands will have a lot more outs.*

Example 4

Andrew

Barry

Barry's pair of nines is beating Andrew's pair of threes. Andrew has just two outs – the missing threes. A spade will give him a flush, but that would not help as Barry's Q♠ will give him a higher flush. Note that Barry has an irrelevant draw to a straight with any jack giving him Q-J-10-9-8. He is winning anyway, so he doesn't need to improve.

> *WARNING: Low pairs that receive no immediate help on the flop are very poor holdings as they are often playing with just two outs.*

Example 5

Andrew

Barry

Andrew is winning with a pair of nines. Barry has six outs: three aces and three queens will give him a higher pair.

Example 6

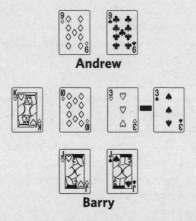

Andrew

Barry

Barry is winning with a pair of jacks against a pair of nines. Andrew has just two outs – the two missing nines.

> *WARNING: Pairs, especially big pairs, are often good hands to play, but if you are losing to a higher pair you are in bad shape, as it is difficult to improve to a stronger hand.*

Developing a feel

Now that we have played through a number of deals you should have some feel for how a hand can develop. However, you will need to refine this further. Rather than filling up the book with hundreds of further examples, I suggest that you get a deck of cards and spend a couple of hours just dealing out hands.

Pretend that you are playing heads-up and expose both your hand and that of your "opponent". Of course, hold'em isn't played like this, but the exercise will be a good one for you to further refine your feel for how hands develop and improve – or don't as the case may be.

You can start by just dealing out all the cards randomly. However, you will only actually play around 20-25 per cent of the hands that you are dealt, and so if you just give yourself and your opponent random cards you will witness a number of rather pointless battles between hands such as 9♣-2♥ and 6♦-J♠.

I would therefore suggest that after a while you deal out more natural starting hands and play out a number of deals with these starting hands fixed. This will also give you a good feel for how certain hands tend to get on against certain other hands. I would suggest the following battles:

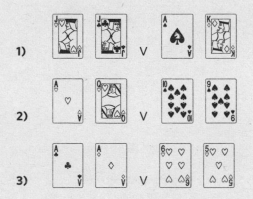

57

4)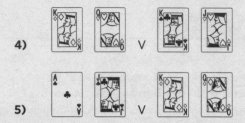

5)

In each case give the first hand to yourself, the latter hand to your "opponent" and then play out the deal in the standard way: three flop cards, then the turn and finally the river. Repeat this about 20 times for each pairing. Note that in each case you have the better starting hand. View the play with the following thoughts:

1) What sort of flops are good for me?
2) If I get a good flop, how often am I getting outdrawn by the river?
3) If the flop is bad and I get outdrawn, how often can I turn it around by the river?

Chapter 5

Hold'em play: basic principles

Before discussing how to play specific hands in the pre-flop stage, I would like to introduce various concepts crucial to the understanding of what you are trying to achieve when playing hold'em.

Odds and pot odds

I have occasionally mentioned probabilities in the earlier text. However, now that we are about to get into the nitty-gritty of hold'em play we need to formalise exactly what is meant by odds, and also to introduce the concept of pot odds.

Odds

The odds of a particular event are a representation of the chances of it happening and are expressed as x-to-y where, more often than not, y is 1. The "y" is the chance that the event will happen and "x" is the chance that it won't. Thus, if you roll a normal dice the chance that a six will appear is 5-to-1 – there is one chance that it will happen and five chances that it won't. If you shuffle a pack of cards, cut them and then look at the top card, the chance that it will be an ace is 12-to-1.

Odds are crucial in all forms of poker, and poker texts constantly discuss odds in numerous different situations. For example, if you have two clubs and the flop comes with precisely two clubs, then you have a flush draw. What are the odds of this flush being completed on the turn?

There are 52 cards in the deck and you can see five of them. There are thus 47 unseen cards. Nine of these (the missing clubs) are helpful and will complete your draw; 38 are unhelpful and will not. Thus your chances of completing your flush draw on the turn are 38-to-9. This expression is rather unwieldy but it is fairly close to 4-to-1. Thus your chances are about 1 in 5 or about 20 per cent. An approximation such as this will be fine for real-life decisions.

Pot odds

The discussion of odds leads naturally on to considerations of pot odds. Pot odds basically represent the amount of money you have to put into the pot to call a bet relative to the amount of money currently in the pot. Thus if there is $30 in the pot and you need to call a bet of $10 you are receiving pot odds of 3-to-1. If there is $100 in the pot and you have to call a bet of $20 your pot odds are 5-to-1.

There are many decisions in hold'em which are purely dependent upon the pot odds that you are receiving.

Here is a simple example:

Flop

Your Hand

Here you have a flush draw and there is one card remaining to be dealt. There is $80 in the pot, you have just one opponent and they bet $10. You are "certain" that they hold either an ace or a king in their hand, so your only chance to win the pot is by completing your flush – making a pair of queens or nines will be no good. Should you call?

To work out the answer we need to calculate the odds of completing our draw and then consider the pot odds. We do not have to do this to six decimal places – a rough estimate will be fine. From our previous calculations we know that the odds of completing a flush draw with just one card are approximately 4-to-1. Here we are being offered pot odds of 8-to-1. The pot odds are very much better than our actual odds and we should call.

If the pot were instead much smaller at just $30 and the bet remained at $10 then our pot odds are just 3-to-1. This is worse than the 4-to-1 chance of completing our flush and we should fold.

If you are not convinced of this look what happens if we play each scenario out five times.

Firstly the pot is $80 and we call for $10. With average luck we will make our flush one time in five. Thus on four occasions we will simply lose the $10 we have invested while on the other occasion we will hit and end up winning $80. Thus our bet (actually call, to be precise) shows a profit of $40 in five outings or an average of $8 per play.

We can make a similar calculation when the pot is $30 and now we see that - over five attempts - we will still lose $40. However, our win will be worth only $30 and so we will end up $10 down over five plays. Thus, now our call has a negative expectation of $2 per play and we are better off folding.

Note that folding in the first example would be a big mistake, whereas calling in the second example is a much smaller mistake.

Typical Drawing Hands

Here are some typical drawing situations and their odds. Hopefully by now you will be able to recognise these drawing situations and have a good feel for the number of outs each hand holds.

Obviously you can never precisely know your opponent's hand, but situations frequently arise in which it is pretty clear how many cards are likely to win the pot for you.

Flush draw with overcards
Example:

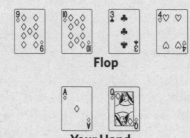

Flop

Your Hand

Your opponent holds: a pair and kicker below queens, eg J-10
Number of outs: 15
Exact chance to hit: 31-to-15
Rough approximation: 2-to-1

Open-ended straight draw
Example:

Flop

Your Hand

Your opponent holds: a high pair, eg A-K
Number of outs: 8
Exact chance to hit: 38-to-8
Rough approximation: 5-to-1

Two overcards
Example:

Flop

Your Hand

Your opponent holds: a pair lower than kings, eg J-10
Number of outs: 6
Exact chance to hit: 40-to-6
Rough approximation: 7-to-1

Gutshot Draw
Example:

Flop

Your Hand

Your opponent holds: any remotely decent pair!
Number of outs: 4
Exact chance to hit: 42-to-4
Rough approximation: 10-to-1

Implied odds

When we consider pot odds we are looking at a specific situation – it costs a certain amount to call a bet and there is a certain amount of money in the pot. This generates a specific "value" for our bet. However, there are occasions when you will want to call a bet even though you are sure that you are currently losing and the current pot odds do not justify a call. Such situations rely on implied odds.

Consider the following:

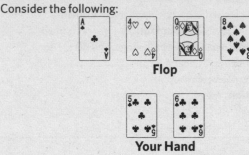

Flop

Your Hand

Let's assume there is $90 in the pot and it is $10 to call your opponent's bet. Your opponent has bet the hand strongly and you know he has a decent hand – probably a high pair. Your only chance is to complete your gutshot with a seven. Should you call the bet?

Working strictly on pot odds we calculate as follows. It is most unlikely that our opponent has a seven (he almost certainly has two high cards) so there are four winning cards for us out of 44 unseen cards. This generates odds of 40-to-4 or 10-to-1. The pot is offering us odds of 9-to-1. Therefore we should fold.

However, if we call the bet and the miracle seven does indeed appear on the river, consider what will happen. Our opponent will not be worried, as it will be hard for him to believe that this innocent-looking seven could possibly have helped us. He will therefore bet. We have the nut hand and raise. He will probably call this bet and will thus end up losing a total of $20 on the river. So, in addition to the $90 that was in the pot on the turn we have accumulated an extra $20 when we hit our seven (if we don't hit the seven it doesn't matter – we will fold on the river and will not lose any more money). This makes a total of $110. So, you could argue that the true pot odds for the call on the turn were 11-to-1 and not 9-to-1. As we already know, the chance of completing our hand is 10-to-1 and so now the call has a positive rather than a negative value. This is what implied odds are all about – the implication that you can make more money than is currently in the pot when you do hit your hand. Implied odds are also an important concept in pre-flop play – as we shall soon see.

> *TIP: Do not get carried away trying to calculate with precise accuracy the benefits of any play involving pot odds and/or implied odds. Many of them are borderline. The important thing is to understand the principle so that you avoid wildly incorrect decisions.*

Position

Position is an absolutely fundamental concept in hold'em. The key point with hold'em is that your position (with regards to when the betting comes to you) is fixed throughout the entire deal. If you have bad position (ie the betting comes to you early in the action) then you are stuck with it for the whole hand. If you are in the favourable situation of having late position, then this is an advantage you carry with you for the whole hand. In this respect the game differs from stud where the player who is obliged to open the betting can change from round to round.

The only slight exception to the fact that position is absolutely fixed in hold'em is with regard to the blinds. On the pre-flop round of betting the blinds are in the advantageous position of being last to speak. However, on all post-flop rounds the blinds will speak first.

It is a great advantage to have good position and it can result in saving bets that would otherwise have been lost, and gaining bets which might have slipped through your fingers if you had bad position. Let's see how this works in practice.

What happens with bad position

Imagine that after the pre-flop play there are four players left in the pot including you. You are first to speak. The flop comes down and you like the look of it – so you bet. The second player now raises, the third player calls and the fourth player now re-raises. With all this heavy action your holding suddenly appears a lot less attractive and – rather than call two more bets (the raise and the re-raise) you decide to fold. However, this cost you a bet because you opened the betting.

Next time you are in this position you decide to play more circumspectly and you check. Your plan is that if the action heats up before it gets round to you, you will fold. However, it turns out that nobody has very much and the round gets checked out. Now the turn card is dealt and it is a bad one for you. It does nothing for your hand but has helped one of your opponents to overtake you. Bad news. However, if you had bet the flop in the first place this player would have had to fold and you would have gone on to win the pot, but you are not psychic and you didn't know that.

What happens with good position

Now look what happens if you are in late position and the same two scenarios occur. In the first example, the opposition have some good hands; someone bets early on and there is a caller and then before the action gets to you there is a raise. Now you get the message, you discard your hand and you didn't waste a bet.

The second example also works in your favour. You have your moderate hand and are not entirely sure if you want to bet it or not. However, before you make your decision you see all three of your three opponents checking. It is therefore likely that no-one has very much, and so you decide your moderate hand is worth a bet. It turns out that they do indeed not have very much, they all fold and you take the pot. The player who got lucky first time round never gets a chance this time. He was obliged to reveal that his hand was weak (he checked) and you bet him out of the pot.

> *TIP: In poker, as with many things in life, information is power. When you have good position you gain information, when you have bad position you don't.*

Chapter 6

Pre-flop play: general principles

Position and pre-flop play

In the previous chapter we looked at the idea of position, and saw how it can be a very important factor for the play of hands. Position is also critical in pre-flop play, and having bad position is again a serious drawback. The fact that you have to make decisions about betting before knowing anything else about any of the other hands at the table means that you need a very strong hand to get involved. As your position improves around the table, this requirement becomes less stringent and you can then play more hands.

The concept of position is something that many beginning players find hard to understand. They will happily join in the game with all kinds of feeble holdings in early position, as they realise that given a helpful enough flop then "any two cards can win".

> *WARNING: Playing bad hands out of position is probably the single worst error that is made by weak hold'em players.*

In order to understand why it is just so bad to play weak hands in early position, consider the following.

The game of 100

Let us invent a new game which bears a passing similarity to hold'em. As with hold'em, there are ten players around the table, but instead of a pack of playing cards we are using a "pack" of 100 cards with the numbers 1 to 100 on them. The pack is shuffled and each player is dealt one card. As with hold'em there will be a round of betting, during which players may fold, call, or even raise. There will only be one round of betting. When the betting is complete, there will be a showdown and the player with the highest card will win.

Let us imagine that you are now first to speak. How good would your card have to be before you decide to bet?

You know that you have to beat nine other random cards, so you need something pretty good – what do you think that would be? 85? 90? Perhaps even 92 or 93?

There is no doubt a mathematical formula which can give you the exact point at which you should bet rather than fold, but I think that most players would intuitively feel that they needed to hold at least number 90 to risk a bet.

Now let us imagine that five players have already folded so there are only four other random hands for you to beat. Now how high a card would you need? 80? Maybe just a little more – perhaps 83? Again I am sure a mathematical formula could generate the "correct" figure, but it should be obvious that this number will be a fair bit less than the number needed if you had to open the betting from early position.

Now let us assume that seven players have folded and you have just two opponents. Now you might take a chance with something quite a bit lower, maybe just 70, or even 65. You will also notice that now another possibility arises. With quite a poor number, say just 35, you might consider betting anyway on the grounds that your two opponents might not have very high numbers and might just fold. Thus you might bet with 35 and the next player, holding a 45, might fold and you could get to take the pot with your "bluff". Such a strategy was less attractive when you had more opponents as then there was obviously a greater chance that you would run into a powerhouse with someone holding a really big number such as 98, 99 or even 100. As the number of opponents decreases, so does the possibility that there is a big card out against you.

Obviously this "game" is a very crude approximation to hold'em. In hold'em there will be post-flop play and any holding can then beat any other holding with a favourable flop. However, the important principle is that when you get involved in a pot you should do so in circumstances that give you a good chance to be (initially at least) holding the best hand. If you are constantly entering pots with insufficiently strong hands relative to your position, you will find yourself involved in endless uphill struggles.

Without wishing to sound overly dramatic, when you enter a pot, you make a decision that you are going to war. If you are going to war you want to make sure that there is an excellent chance that your weapons are stronger than those of your opponents. If you commence hostilities armed with a pea-shooter and your opponent unleashes a bazooka, you are going to get blown away more often than not.

Domination

Another key concept in hold'em pre-flop play is that of domination. Some hands dominate other hands which makes it hard for the weaker hand to overtake the stronger one. Let's consider some examples.

1) Your opponent holds 9-9 and you hold Q-J

Your opponent currently has a stronger hand than you, but your hand is not dominated. Any jack or queen will give you a pair higher than you opponent's nines and will improve you to the winning hand. Your opponent is a slight favourite; if the hand is played out to the river the chances are approximately 55 per cent-45 per cent in favour of your opponent.

2) Your opponent holds A-J and you hold K-Q

As before, you are behind, but your hand is not dominated. Kings and queens are outs for you – both your cards are "live". If the hand is played out to the river the chances are approximately 60 per cent-40 per cent in your opponent's favour.

3) Your opponent holds 9-9 and you hold A-6

Now you are partially dominated. An ace will help you but a six won't. This is a poor situation. In hold'em you want both of your cards to be working for you and here the six is a bit of a passenger and you are really just playing with an ace. Your opponent is a good favourite; if the hand is played out to the river the chances are approximately 70 per cent-30 per cent in favour of your opponent.

4) Your opponent holds 9-9 and you hold 7-6

Now your hand is badly dominated. Hitting either a six or a seven on its own is not going to help you as it merely gives you a pair weaker than your opponent's nines. You will need to see a substantial improvement on the board in order to overtake your opponent. You will need something like 7-6, 6-6, 7-7 or an unlikely straight to materialise – and all of these are longshots. Your opponent is a big favourite; if the hand is played out to the river the chances are approximately 85 per cent-15 per cent in your opponent's favour.

There are two other common situations where domination occurs:

1) A higher pair versus a lower pair, eg K-K v J-J

Now the weaker hand probably needs to hit one of only two missing jacks to improve to the best hand. The jacks are badly dominated. If the hand is played to the river the higher pair triumphs by approximately 82 per cent-18 per cent.

2) A shared card, eg A-Q v Q-10

Here the weaker hand is reduced to trying to hit a ten, as pairing the queen will also make a pair for the stronger side who will then have the better kicker. This is again a very good situation for the stronger hand which will come out on top by a ratio of approximately 72 per cent-28 per cent.

Small cards

In general you want to play big cards in hold'em. This should be obvious – big cards can make big hands: big pairs, big two pairs, big sets, top straights, big full houses etc. Small cards make small hands, are easily dominated and tend to lose to big hands. Thus, there is a very simple rule about small cards:

> **WARNING: Very simple rule to remember about small cards: do not play them!**

In lower limit hold'em games many players flout this rule and will happily enter the pot with 7♣-6♣, 4♥-3♥, 9♦-8♥, J♠-8♠. Occasionally they will get lucky and make a straight or a flush and win a decent-sized pot. Short term this will be a good result, but long term it is a disaster as it will encourage them to play such cards again.

There are so many problems with playing small cards that it is hard to know where to start, but let's try anyway. A holding like 8♣-7♣ can be playable in certain circumstances, but if you are consistently playing it against stronger hands you will run into all sorts of trouble.

Typical small card problems

Let's consider problems that arise when you have a hand like 8♣-7♣ that do not arise when you have a solid hand such as K♣-Q♣.

1) You hit a pair on the flop

When you make a pair on the flop, it is always good if you have top pair, ie if there are three cards of different rank, then your pair is formed by matching the top card. If you do not have top pair, you will always face tricky decisions as you can never be sure whether someone else has made a higher pair. With K♣-Q♣ it is quite likely that you will have top pair as the only possible overcard is an ace. Thus your only difficult hands will be ones with quite specific flops such as A-Q-7 or A-K-2. Of course, you can make top pair and have a very good kicker and still be losing, but at least you will not have difficult decisions to make during the play. You will bet the hand hard and it will just be bad luck when you lose.

However, when you make a pair with 8♣-7♣, there will nearly always be an overcard (or overcards) and it will be much harder to know where you stand. Consider flops such as K-8-3, Q-7-4 or J-10-8. In all cases you have a pair, but the flops are dangerous for you because there are overcards to your pair on the board which may well have enabled players to make bigger pairs than you.

Consider the final case – J-10-8.

Flop

Your Hand

Although there are two overcards to your pair, you might think this looks quite good because you also have a chance to make a straight if a nine arrives. However, note that a nine will generate the sequence J-10-9-8-7. This will indeed give you a straight, but it will be beaten by anyone who has a queen in their hand as they will now have a higher straight (their Q-J-10-9-8 will beat your J-10-9-8-7).

There is a further point here. Another of your improving cards is a seven which will give you two pair. However, if a seven comes on the board then J-10-8-7 has materialised and an opponent needs only a nine to complete a straight. This is typical of what can happen when you play small cards. You are running the risk of making second-best hands where you will feel obliged to pay off the stronger hand.

2) You flop a Really Good Hand
Even when you hit wonderful flops you will still face problems when you play low cards. Here is an example.

You have 8♣-7♣ and the flop is J♠-10♥-9♥.

Flop

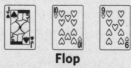

Your Hand

Wonderful! You have flopped a straight. Surely this is fantastic and justifies your speculative play with the low cards? No – it doesn't. You can lose from this position surprisingly easily. If a seven comes, anyone with an eight will tie; if an eight comes, anyone with a queen will beat you and anyone with a seven will tie; if a queen comes, anyone with a king will beat you and anyone with an eight will tie; if a king comes, anyone with a queen will beat you. If you have many opponents, you will be quite fortunate if your hand is still good at the river. Consider this: with just one opponent, holding Q♥-J♦ you are "only" a 2-to-1 favourite to win by the river.

Let's assume that instead you had played stronger cards and started with K♣-Q♣. Now you have still flopped a straight but you have a rock solid hand. Critically, you have the higher end of the straight. You will be unlucky if queens and/or kings arrive, but even then you will still probably split the pot. Suddenly an eight becomes a great card for you.

Flop

Your Hand

Anyone with a seven might stick around with their low straight, whereas a player with a queen will have a straight, but you will have a stronger one (theirs goes up to the queen but yours goes up to the king). You can make a lot of money with your hand.

However, despite all of this, low cards are occasionally playable, but it has to be in exactly the right circumstances. As a beginning player you could adopt the following very crude rule about pre-flop play – you will only consider playing your hand if:

1) You have a pocket pair or
2) If both of you cards are ten or higher.
Everything else you will fold.

I am not going to recommend that you play like this but, if you did, you would be making very few mistakes.

Entering the pot

There are three basic ways that the play can come to you in the pre-flop betting round:

1) No-one has yet entered the pot.
2) One or more players have called (limped).
3) Someone has opened with a raise (and there may be callers)
Let's consider each in turn.

1) No-one has yet entered the pot
Everyone in the hand so far has folded and the action comes to you. As we know you have a choice here – you can open with a raise, you can just call (limp) or you can fold. Which you will want to do depends on the strength of your hand and your position. When you have a very strong hand, such as a big pair or two very high cards, you will want to open with a raise. This forces other players (with the exception of the blinds) to pay a double bet to stay in the pot. If you just limp then it

becomes cheap for players to see the flop with weaker hands and one of them might get lucky and outdraw you. If you have a big hand and other players want to play their speculative hands, then you must charge them a premium to do so.

There is a further reason why you usually want to open with a raise – it gives you a chance to win the pot immediately. Raising puts pressure on the opposition. If everyone folds you win the pot at once (winning the blind money). This is rarely a bad thing. If you limp there are two problems: firstly, it is cheaper for other players to compete; secondly, the small blind (who is already half in) can get a cheap look at the flop, while the big blind gets a completely free look at the flop.

Situations where you consider limping are where you have a moderate hand which has the potential to become very good but needs a helpful flop. In such cases you are hoping to see the flop cheaply and actually welcome the participation of other players. Firstly, it boosts the pot size and secondly, if you do get lucky and make a big hand you want someone else to make a decent – but second-best – hand and pay you off.

If you are in late or even middle position then you should not open limp. You are less worried about there being a monster hand out against you, and you want to maximise your chances of winning at once. The possibility of winning immediately is such an important consideration that if you want to play from middle or late position it is best to raise.

> **TIP: Limping will encourage the participation of other players and may create a multi-way pot. Raising will keep the numbers down.**

2) One or more players have called (limped)

If you are going to play and other players have already entered the pot, then you can raise or just limp along with everyone else. Players who have limped into the pot generally have moderate hands, so if you have a powerful hand you should raise and the others will probably call. Now your powerful hand will have less chance of standing up than if you had been in a position to open raise with it and drive these other players out. However, with more players there will be more money in the middle, so when you do win (and this will be often) you will take down a big pot.

If you have a moderate hand with good drawing possibilities, this is a good time to join in the limping. You will want to hit the flop hard so that you are not really worried about your hand being dominated. For example if you call after two or three limpers with J♠-10♠ there is a serious danger that you are dominated by one or maybe even two other players. However, you are not really looking to make a pair and have it hold up with a hand like this. That can happen, but basically you are after bigger fish. You are hoping to flop a straight or flush draw and make a lot of money if it comes in.

3) Someone has opened with a raise

If an early position player opens with a raise you need a major hand to compete. If you have such a hand and you want to play, then you will usually re-raise. Many weak players do not understand this principle and you will see them calling pre-flop raises with all sorts of hands, some very good, some relatively weak.

If you think about this, it is obvious why you should raise or fold. Someone has opened with a raise. If they are a sensible player then clearly they should have a strong hand. Now:

1) Your hand is weaker

If your hand is likely to be weaker than your opponent's, you should fold. You have no idea how many other players will join in (if any) so you cannot judge whether you have any implied odds. Paying a lot of money to compete against a stronger hand is not smart poker.

2) Your hand is stronger

If you really think your hand is stronger then it is quite likely that your hand dominates that of the raiser (eg they have A-J and you have A-K). Now your ideal scenario is to take on the raiser heads up, when you will be in an excellent position. Your hand might even hold up if it doesn't improve – a scenario which is most unlikely if there are more players involved. Re-raising creates a good chance to generate this situation. Now other players will have to pay three bets to play (slightly less for the blinds) and they are liable to shy away unless they have a serious hand. You are in a good position and you do not want other drawing hands coming along and confusing the issue.

If a middle or late position player opens with a raise, then the situation is slightly different. Such players do not need such a good hand to open with, and so you can loosen your requirements for taking them on. However, again – if you want to play you should usually raise. The reasons you took on an early raiser with a re-raise still apply here.

An exception to this raising strategy occurs when there has been an open raise and one or more calls. Now you might be able to get good value with a call for a decent drawing hand such as 8-8 or K-Q suited.

TIP: If you see a player who is often calling raises pre-flop, then they are almost certainly a weak player.

Playing from the blinds

Any time that you are playing from one of the blind positions, your requirements to enter the pot again change. You have already contributed some money to the pot, so it is less expensive for you to now get involved than for other players. This means that your pot odds (and implied odds) will always be better, and this allows you to take more chances with speculative hands in these positions.

This is especially true of the big blind. If there is no raise before the play gets to you then you can take a free play. If there is a single raise then the pot is likely to be fairly big, and you will only have to contribute one bet rather than two to see the flop.

The small blind is slightly less well placed to take advantage of these factors. Firstly, the small blind is (usually) only half a bet, so even with no raises you are still obliged to contribute something to the pot to see the flop. If there has already been a raise then you have to pay $1\frac{1}{2}$ bets, which is 75 per cent of what late position players are paying. Note that as the small blind you are also stuck with the worst possible position for the entire hand.

In summary, if you are in the big blind you can play a fair number of speculative hands against a raiser. This is especially the case if there have also been callers to bump up the pot and thus improve your odds. In the small blind it will be so cheap to see the flop in an unraised pot that you can call with even quite weak hands (note that players calling instead of raising also implies that the hands out against you are weaker). However, to play against a raiser you still need to possess a very good hand.

Chapter 7

Pre-flop play: specific strategies

We have discussed a number of concepts that can arise in hold'em which are relevant to pre-flop play. Now let's consider how they will lead us to assess and play specific hands in specific positions.

Playing pairs

Before discussing the play of pocket pairs pre-flop there is one important statistic which you must know. The chance of hitting a set on the flop (ie a card of the same rank as your pair arriving on the flop and thus giving you three of a kind) is $7\frac{1}{2}$-to-1. Often when you play a pair, your only realistic chance to win the pot is to flop a set. Since this is something of a longshot, you must often make sure that you are getting reasonable pot odds to play your pair.

Top Pairs (A-A, K-K, Q-Q)

These are the very best hands you can get and they will not come along very often. These holdings are so strong that your position at the table becomes irrelevant. When you pick these up, you will bet, raise and re-raise if possible. They are premium hands. You will (nearly always) be the favourite in the pot and you should charge you opponents the maximum to play. Much of the time you will be dominating your opponent's hands. In fact the only situation where this does not happen is when you hold Q-Q and an opponent has A-K (or if you are unlucky enough to run into an overpair).

With A-A you have the best possible hand and with K-K and Q-Q the chance of someone holding a better hand than yours is remote.

What you want to happen

Ideally you would like just one or two opponents seeing the flop with you, with these players paying a premium price to do so. The pot will be a good size and you will be a favourite to win it. Sometimes you will find that you will see the flop with more opponents, maybe four or even five. As long as they have all paid well for the privilege, this is fine for you. You will not win these pots as often as you will with just one or two opponents, but when you do, the pots are likely to be very big.

What you don't want to happen

You do not want to let numerous players see the flop cheaply. This is disastrous. You will have failed to build up a big pot and given yourself the greatest possible chance of being outdrawn. You are less likely to win the pot and, when you do, it is smaller.

Sometimes weaker players like to get fancy with these big hands and play them slowly – limping pre-flop and then maybe even just calling on the flop with the idea of unleashing a big raise on the turn when the bet size doubles. However, limping with these hands pre-flop and allowing other, weaker, hands to see the flop cheaply is a major mistake. You will occasionally land a big pot playing like this, but frequently someone speculating with a drawing hand will outdraw you and you suffer an unnecessary and frustrating loss.

Strong pairs (J-J, 10-10)

These are also excellent holdings. You will nearly always see the flop with these hands, and very often you will be raising and re-raising with them. It is still highly likely that you have the best hand, but now you are less likely to be dominating opponents. If you have J-J an opponent with A-K, A-Q or K-Q has a playable hand. When you hold 10-10 you can add A-J, K-J and Q-J to the mix of hands which will be playable against yours.

You are also much more likely to see overcards on the flop. With Q-Q you are a favourite to dodge overcards on the flop. However, when your pair drops to 10-10 the chance of avoiding overcards is only 30 per cent.

What you want to happen
As with the top pairs, you would again like to see the flop with a small number of opponents, with them paying a premium. With just one or two opponents you may still hold the best hand even if one overcard arrives on the flop. When you have numerous opponents it is likely that any overcard will leave you in trouble. At the very least it will make the hand harder to play.

What you don't want to happen
Same story as with the top pairs. You do not want to let numerous players see the flop cheaply. In principle you don't mind having many opponents – as long as they are paying well for the privilege. If nothing else you will be getting reasonable implied odds to hit a set, and you could also receive a favourable flop of low cards when your pair still has a good chance to stand up.

Medium pairs (9-9, 8-8, 7-7)

These are good hands and are often playable. They are nearly always playable if no-one has yet entered the pot or if one or more players have entered the pot, but with calls (suggesting moderate hands) rather than raises (suggesting powerful hands). They are not generally good hands to play if you suspect that other players have strong hands, as they are dominated by higher pairs.

One problem with these hands is that it is very likely that one or more overcards will arrive on the flop, and this can make them difficult to handle with small numbers of opponents (with a large number of opponents you will usually just give up if you don't flop a set and the board is otherwise unhelpful).

What you want to happen

Medium pairs can generally be profitable in two ways:
1) You see the flop with one or perhaps two opponents at most. Normally you will need to open with a raise to make this happen. Now you have a reasonable chance to win even if your pair does not improve.
2) You see the flop relatively cheaply with numerous opponents. Now you are hoping to flop a set, but you have some chances to win even if you do not.

What you don't want to happen

You do not want to pay a premium price to see the flop with a small number of opponents. You do not want to be in a pot with just one or two opponents if there is strong evidence that one of them has a big hand which might dominate you.

Small pairs (6-6, 5-5, 4-4, 3-3, 2-2)

Unlike the medium pairs, these hands are playable only in certain circumstances. You should not always enter the pot with them as they are just too weak. It is with small pairs that the concept of implied odds (see Chapter 4) really becomes important. When you play these hands and you do not flop a set there will usually be two and maybe even three overcards. If you have more than one opponent in such circumstances it is unlikely that you will be able to continue.

As we already know, the chances of flopping a set are $7\frac{1}{2}$-to-1. If you relied purely on pot odds to decide whether you could play a small pair pre-flop you would almost never enter a pot. It would require that seven opponents had already entered the pot before you and this would be a truly freak occurrence.

These hands rely on implied odds. You look to enter pots cheaply, with reasonable pot odds and then hope to flop a set. If you do then you will have a well-concealed monster hand and a fine chance to win a big pot. In other words – your implied odds will be excellent.

You are generally looking for pot odds of around 4-to-1 or 5-to-1 in a modest-sized pot to be able to play these hands. Thus, in a $5-$10 game if there is $20 in the pot and it costs $5 to call then calling is okay. To get "value" for your call you would need to guarantee winning around $40 when you hit your set. Nothing is ever certain in poker, but it is reasonable to assume that – on average – you will do better than that.

What you want to happen

Small pairs, like medium pairs, can be profitable in two ways:

1) You see the flop heads up with just one opponent who does not necessarily have a strong hand. Now there is a fair chance that you can win unimproved. If your opponent does not make a pair or any kind of draw on the flop then you may win the pot straightaway. If they call along with a weak drawing hand, then they can miss and your small pair may stand up anyway.

2) You see the flop relatively cheaply with numerous opponents. The more the merrier but ideally at least three. Now you are hoping to flop a set. When you do get lucky you can win a very big pot as the strength of your hand will be well disguised. If you miss the set on the flop then, barring some freak event (eg you have 4-4 and the flop is 6-5-3), you are done with the hand and will fold as soon as someone bets. Note that you are not worried about being dominated by a higher pair. Unless you receive an excellent flop you plan to give up anyway.

What you don't want to happen
You do not want to pay a premium price to see the flop with a small number of opponents.

Playing unpaired high cards

Unpaired high cards are the bread-and-butter hands at hold'em. You will be dealt a couple of decent high cards a lot more often than you will receive a pair, and most of the time when you are involved in a pot it will be with unpaired high cards. With such hands you are basically hoping to receive a card on board to give you a pair. As you are playing two high cards, it is likely that you will then have top pair with either the best, or a decent, kicker. This is usually a strong hand, especially if you have just one or two opponents.

If your high cards are suited, this is a small but potentially significant bonus. It gives you a modest chance to make a flush and is of most use when you have many opponents. Any time that you make a flush in these circumstances, you can win a big pot.

The value of high cards changes significantly with regard to position. This is because the possibility of domination. You need to be very cautious about playing high cards from early position and need the absolute best hands to do so. Consider a hand such as Q-J. If four or five players have already folded then it is quite reasonable to open with this hand. However, if you are either first or second to speak, you should just fold with this hand as it is easily dominated by A-Q, A-J, K-Q and K-J. It is also facing an uphill struggle against A-K and all big pairs. If you remember the game of 100, then trying to play Q-J in early position is like betting on the number 80 when you have eight or nine opponents – far too risky and, in the long run, unprofitable.

Strong high card combinations

These are really just A-K and A-Q. If you are in early position, these are the only non-pair hands that you should definitely play and you should raise with them. A-J and K-Q can just about be labelled "strong high card combinations" and you can still open raise with these, especially if they are suited. All other high card combinations, eg A-10, K-J etc are just too weak and vulnerable to domination.

In middle and late position you can again relax your standards. In middle position you can open raise with A-10 and K-J, and in late position you can add Q-J. Other hands such as K-10 and Q-10 are borderline cases.

What you want to happen

Powerful high cards play much like the big pairs. You want a small number of opponents and you want them paying well to see the flop. If you have A-K and face just one opponent (or even two) you can even win pots when your hand doesn't improve. This is most unlikely with more than two opponents. If you can get heads up with a hand that you are dominating then you are in very good shape.

What you don't want to happen

As usual for the big hands you don't want a number of players seeing the flop cheaply with moderate drawing hands.

Moderate high card combinations

These are all hands below A-J and K-Q (it is probably best to regard these as "crossover" hands – they are just about okay to play in early position and certainly okay in middle position). They are A-10, K-J, Q-J, K-10, Q-10 and J-10. Below this and you are getting into the realms of "speculative hands". These moderate high cards are hands that you definitely do not want to play against players who have shown a lot of strength, ie open raisers from early or middle position. There is a very great danger you will be dominated. For example, a hand like K-10 is deceptive. It looks like a good couple of high cards, but it is dominated by numerous hands: A-A, K-K, Q-Q, J-J, 10-10, A-K, A-10, K-Q and K-J.

These hands are generally playable in two situations:

1) If you are down to just three or four opponents, ie middle to late position, then it is okay to open raise with them. There is a reasonable chance that you have the best hand, and the danger of being up against a bigger hand is counterbalanced by the chance that everyone may fold and you might take the blinds straight away.

2) If there have been a couple of callers it is often (not always) okay to call with these hands. There are two other factors that should affect your decision: whether your hand is suited, and your position. These hands play much better in volume pots with good position and – as we have already seen – being suited is a big bonus too.

What you want to happen

You want to take the initiative and play with good position against just one or two opponents. Alternatively you are happy to compete in a multi-way pot if you can get in cheaply. In the latter situation you are greatly helped if your cards are suited and also by having good position.

What you don't want to happen

You do not want to pay a premium price to compete against a very strong hand when there is a great danger of domination.

Speculative hands

Any holding that does not comprise two high cards and is not a pair is a speculative hand. In fact, strictly speaking, a lot of low to medium pairs are speculative hands too, but I have dealt with them in the section on playing pairs.

Speculative hands can have three things going for them:

1) High card strength

2) Suitedness

3) Connectedness

The more of these features that they have, the better the hand. Let's consider each in turn:

High card strength

You may be puzzled by this, as I have already said that speculative hands do not contain high cards. However, do not make the mistake of thinking that all hands that do not contain aces and kings are equal. J-10 is a clearly stronger hand than 8-7 – you have a much better chance of your hand holding up if you make just a pair. In turn, 8-7 is much better than 5-4, for more or less the same reasons. If you are contemplating getting involved with a speculative hand, then the higher the cards the better.

There is another type of speculative hand that has high card strength – a suited ace. If you play a hand such as A♣-6♣, then you are mainly hoping to get in cheap and win a big pot if you make a flush. However, it is also possible that an ace will come on the flop and this may give you the best hand. You have to be very cautious with these A-x hands when you pair the ace, especially if somebody else has got excited about the flop. If they have a decent ace with a good kicker then you are in bad shape.

Suitedness

This should be fairly straightforward. Suited cards give you a chance to make a flush and, as such, are obviously a bonus. The benefits that derive from having suited cards were discussed at length in the previous chapter.

Connectedness

Connected cards offer you chances to make a straight, and the more connected they are the better. The reason for this should be obvious – there are more possible straights to be made. If you have 7-6 you can make four possible straights which use both cards (10-9-8-7-6, 9-8-7-6-5, 8-7-6-5-4 and 7-6-5-4-3). If you have a gap, eg 8-6, this drops to three (10-9-8-7-6, 9-8-7-6-5 and 8-7-6-5-4). With 9-6 and 10-6 the numbers drop to two and one respectively. Note that the straightening value of cards drops off when they get really low. For example 3-4 can only make three straights using both cards. The straight up to the four doesn't exist. The same applies at the opposite end of the food chain as K-Q and Q-J (for example) are limited in the number of straights which they can make. As you will doubtless have realised, this is no big deal as you are not really playing those cards for their straightening value in the first place.

> *NOTE: A combination such as 8-6 or 9-7 is known as a one-gapper. As you might expect, 7-4 and 9-6 are two-gappers.*

Speculative hands can be playable if no-one has shown much strength. They are also sometimes playable from the big blind (and the small blind in unraised pots) if the pot odds are attractive.

> *WARNING: You need to be quite choosy about when you play speculative hands. If you pick the right circumstances they offer good value. However, many weak players' eyes light up when they see 7♣-6♣ and they will play this hand in any position at any time. This is a big leak.*

What you want to happen

With a speculative hand you want to get in cheaply when it looks like there will be a lot of players in the pot. It helps if you have good position.

What you don't want to happen

As usual you don't want to be in two- or three-player pots up against big hands.

Chapter 8

Post-flop concepts

Introduction

If you have read through the previous material and understood it, then you are by now about 75 per cent of the way towards being a decent player at the low limits. If you are playing a $1-$2 game or a $2-$4 game and you can play well at the pre-flop stage then – even if your post-flop play is poor – you are probably going to be at least a break-even player. However, your post-flop play is not going to be poor. In this section we are going to look at how you handle your cards once the flop arrives and how to play the turn and the river.

Pre- and post-flop play

Hold'em divides quite neatly into pre- and post-flop play in a manner similar to how bridge divides into the auction and the play of the hand. In bridge the auction is susceptible (within reason) to exact analysis in much the same way that pre-flop hold'em play can be analysed in great technical detail. Anyone so inclined can memorise tables which denote the "correct" play in virtually all situations. Many books offer readers such tables and imply that memorising them will lead to perfect pre-flop play. I have chosen not to do this in this book, as I believe that understanding what you are trying to achieve pre-flop is of more relevance than learning tables.

Once the flop appears, a similar situation arises to when the auction is complete in bridge and the play of the cards begins. You can still find strong technical players, but there is now much more room for imagination and making plays. It is fairly common to come across hold'em players who have horrible pre-flop standards (and are thus constantly handicapping themselves in their games) but nevertheless actually play rather well after the flop. They have a good feel for what is going on and understand what they and the other players at the table are trying to do.

The flop and the turn

Most books make a clear distinction between flop and turn play and discuss them more or less separately. However, I am not sure this is the best way to consider the play in hold'em as the two are very closely related. I think it makes more sense to break up the play into the following three sections: pre-flop play; flop and turn play; and finally river play.

This seems to me to be more logical. The three sections break down (crudely) as follows.

The play of a hold'em hand

1) Pre-flop play decides whether you are going to get involved in the hand or not.

2) Flop and turn play dictates how the deal plays out when everyone still has chances to improve their hands.

3) River play is rather different in that all the cards are now out and you either have the best hand or you don't.

Furthermore, it is quite common to make a play on the flop in order to prepare a particular play on the turn.

This is another reason for considering the two rounds together.

However, there are two important distinctions between flop and turn play.

Distinctions between flop and turn play

1) The bet size on the turn doubles. As we know, in a $5-$10 game the betting unit on the flop is $5, increasing to $10 for the turn (and river).

2) When the flop arrives you have two further chances to improve your hand; after the turn just one remains. This makes pot odds calculations very different.

The arrival of the flop

The arrival of the flop is really the key moment in a hold'em hand. You already know your two cards and now, in one fell swoop, three of the five board cards arrive. Thus, pre-flop you knew two of the final seven cards (29 per cent). Now you know five of the final seven cards (71 per cent). This is a huge increase in information.

The value of a hand changes dramatically when the three board cards come down. Hands which were very strong pre-flop can suddenly be left looking rather feeble, while modest pre-flop holdings can turn into monsters. Being able to judge where you stand in a hand at this point is a key skill in hold'em.

The arrival of the flop can be a very frustrating time as it is a sad fact that most flops miss most hands. Many players play perfectly well pre-flop but become enveloped by a fog when the flop comes down. They have waited a long time to pick up a decent hand and now they have one and they have pushed it hard pre-flop. They are now in the mood for a fight and they are not going to let a few lousy board cards dampen their enthusiasm. No sir. Sometimes it can be possible to push hands hard which have missed the flop but doing so blindly is a recipe for disaster.

Having said that, it must be emphasised that when you have what appears to you to be good hand you must play actively.

Aggression

All good poker players play actively. Some are merely aggressive, others are very aggressive and some are super-aggressive. One thing you won't hear people saying about a world champion player is: "Boy, is he good – he really creates problems for his opponents by being cautious at just the right time."

In poker, as in life, if you want to be successful you have to make things happen for you. This is done by taking the initiative in pots: betting and raising rather than checking and calling. In post-flop play (and pre-flop for that matter), it is absolutely crucial that you play aggressively. There is no winning style of play that relies on passively responding to your opponents' play.

Getting paid

Limit hold'em is, at heart, a rather technical game. Those of you whose main exposure to poker is via Hollywood films may regard the game as a tremendous battle of egos, where winners can triumph by sheer force of personality. If you are competing live in a major tournament playing no-limit hold'em then there is an element of this in the play. In no-limit hold'em you can bet any amount of money at any time. This means that it is possible to run huge bluffs and bully weak opponents. However, in an anonymous online limit hold'em game such factors are almost completely irrelevant. The amount you can bet at any point in the hand is fixed and so the possibility of shoving all your chips into the pot while eyeballing your opponent is not open to you.

Why do better players beat weaker players at limit hold'em? There are many possible answers but there are two very key reasons:

Why better players win at limit hold'em

1) They win more money with their winning hands.

2) They lose less money with their losing hands.

That's it. That's more or less all there is to it. When a good player has a good hand they know how to push it hard and extract the maximum from their good cards. When they have a good hand but someone else has a better one, they can see the danger and avoid losing as much as a weaker player will.

Why do better players win more money?

1) How do good players win more money with their good hands? They bet and they raise.

2) What do weaker players do that costs them money? They check and they call.

Sometimes it is the correct strategy to check and call. However, this is not very often. If you have a good hand then you should be betting and raising. I cannot emphasise this enough. Even if you play badly, but aggressively, it is very much harder for players to beat you than if you play badly but passively.

When strong limit hold'em players are eyeing up games, what really makes them salivate are players who play passively. Such players are easy to push around. When they hold good hands they let you come along cheaply so that you have chances to outdraw them, and when they have bad hands they happily come along, calling your bets and hoping that something will turn up. Make sure you do not play like this – it is a foolproof strategy for being a loser.

> *WARNING: There are some games where it is possible to win playing a conservative strategy: you can win a tennis match from the baseline and you can have a successful football team that is based on a rock-solid defence. You cannot do this in poker. You simply cannot be a long-term winner if you play a safety-first game. It is not possible.*

Assessing the flop

When considering pre-flop play there are usually specific solutions to specific problems. When you have a decent grasp of the principles involved then the correct play in different situations becomes fairly clear. You have just two cards and your opponents have just two cards. They have either bet them or they haven't. With some experience you can get a good handle on how strong your hand is vis à vis the competition.

Post-flop play is much more slippery. Suddenly there are a lot more variables to consider and a lot more questions that need asking. Pre-flop you are really only asking one question: "Do I belong in this pot?" When the flop comes you need to consider:

Flop questions

1) How good is this flop for me?

2) Is it likely to be good for other players?

3) If it is good, should I bet and/or raise or should I just call?

4) If I have a little something but suspect other players have better hands, then do I have pot odds/implied odds to play?

5) If it is bad, can I justify hanging around or should I just give up?

6) How many opponents do I have, and is that good or bad?

You also need to remember how players (including you) entered the pot in the pre-flop round.

What happened pre-flop?

1) Did they bet and/or raise – implying strong holdings?

2) Did they limp – implying weak holdings?

3) Did they open the betting – implying a solid hand?

4) Did they only join in when one or more others had already called – possibly implying more speculative holdings?

5) Did they get a free/cheap play from the blinds – now they could hold absolutely any cards?

6) Did I show strength pre-flop – will players expect me to have a good hand?

That's a lot to think about and there is no straightforward A-B-C way to play. For the moment we will just look at some flops and decide how well they coordinate with our cards and where we think we might stand. For the moment we will not worry about how we will bet the hands (if at all). We just want to assess the impact of the flop. We will worry about the betting later.

Example 1

You are on the button with K♥-K♠. A middle player limps and the cut-off calls. You raise, the big blind calls, as do the middle player and the cut-off. Four of you see the flop. Let's now judge the following flops.

1a)

This is a great flop. You have an overpair and the flop is completely uncoordinated. It is very difficult for someone to have a stronger hand than you – the only likely holdings to achieve this are 7-7 and 2-2. Furthermore, players who might want to continue do not have many outs against you. Hands like Q-J and 8-7 are playing five outs, whereas something like 3-3 has just two. You can play this hand confidently.

You are not really worried about having many opponents here. It is so difficult for someone to have a better hand than you.

1b)

This is a dangerous flop. The three board cards are very coordinated and there is also a two-flush. You should still have the best hand but it is not out of the question that you are already behind. Your opponents were all limping pre-flop, so hands like J-10 and 10-8 are possible. Furthermore, hands that have connected with the flop suddenly have an awful lot more outs against you than in 1a. For example, 10♥-9♥ has 13 outs, Q♦-J♥ has 9 outs and A♣-5♣ has 12 outs. Proceed cautiously.

This is a flop where you would very much like to have as few opponents as possible. Just one other player could easily miss this flop, but as more players are in the pot it becomes increasingly likely that someone has got a good piece of it.

1c)

This is a bad flop. If someone has just an ace in their hand you are playing just two outs.

Of course you have no way of knowing if there is an ace out against you, but the fact that there might be acts as a brake on your ambitions. If you bet and war breaks out you will have to fold. If you bet and other players come along for the ride you will be faced with difficult decisions.

Example 2

An early player opens with a raise and a middle player calls. The button also calls, as does the small blind. You are in the big blind with Q♠-10♠ and – with pot odds of 9-to-1 – make a perfectly reasonable call. Five of you see the flop.

> *NOTE: When we discussed pre-flop play, I indicated that it was usually poor play to call pre-flop raises and that doing it consistently was certainly bad. You know this, but many of your opponents won't – or if they do they will not heed this advice. In your games you will often find one or more players happily calling pre-flop raises.*

2a)

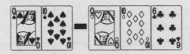

This is a fantastic flop. You have top two pair and are in great shape. You have even overtaken the early raiser if they were playing A-A or

K-K. If someone has A-Q or K-Q they have what appears to them to be a very good hand, but in reality they have just three outs against you. Your main worry is that another high card will appear which could allow someone to overtake you. For example, a jack means that Q-J and A-K (straight) now beat you, whereas a king or ace leaves you vulnerable to straights while someone with two pair using high cards now has a better two pair than you.

2b)

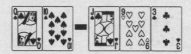

This is a pretty decent flop. You have an open-ended straight draw, giving you eight good outs. You also have a small chance to make a flush as there is one spade on the board. Finally you have an overcard, but I wouldn't get too excited about this. There was an early raiser and a couple of callers, so there are some good hands out there. The main value of your hand is with the straight draw.

2c)

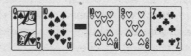

You have top pair, good kicker which is often a very strong hand. Here, however, it is not worth a great deal. The pre-flop raiser may well have an overpair to the board, and any number of the three callers could also find this board attractive. You are badly behind against hands such as K-10 and A-10. Furthermore, the board is rather coordinated with the 7, 9 and 10 all within touching distance, making straight draws possible. Finally, there is a two-flush which also harms your chances. This is the kind of flop where the winning hand is likely to be more than just a pair. Although you have caught the flop to the extent that you have made top pair, your hand does not coordinate well with the flop for the purpose of making better hands such as straights and flushes.

With a flop like this, the number of opponents you have is critical. If you had just one opponent (for example there is a raise from a middle position player, everyone folds and you call from the big blind), then your hand is looking pretty good. They might have caught a good piece of the flop but then again they might not have. However, as the number of opponents increases, so does the danger that this flop poses.

2d)

This is the kind of flop that encourages weak players to dribble away their money. With four opponents, all of whom should have decent hands, this second pair hand is worth very little. If someone has A-A, 10-10 or A-10 you have no outs at all. However, even more modest holdings give you few reasons to be cheerful. A-K and A-J leave you with five outs, while A-Q leaves you trying to hit two outs (the missing tens). This is a decent-sized pot and you might think it is worth hanging around to try and improve, but there is a further problem in that even a queen might not make you a winning hand (it won't if an opponent has A-Q, K-J or even Q-Q (the last being, admittedly, unlikely). I know your opponents can't have everything, but they will turn up with such hands more often than you expect. Chasing outs that merely give other players even bigger hands than you is not the way to play good poker.

> *TIP: Whenever you play a speculative hand against a number of opponents who have shown strength, you are really looking to make more than just a pair. You won't do this very often, which is precisely why they are speculative hands.*

Example 3

You are UTG holding A♥-J♣ and you open with a raise. Everyone folds round to the blinds and they both call. Three of you see the flop.

3a)

This is certainly not a bad flop. You have top pair, good kicker and only two opponents. However, there is a subtle problem with this hand – it is unlikely to make you any money. You have shown strength pre-flop, so your opponents will regard it as likely that you have an ace. So what kind of hand is going to give you action?

Someone with an ace and a weak kicker may elect to come along, but they are not going to get frisky with their hand. Also, note that if a king, queen or nine happens to land on the board then your lovely jack kicker will no longer play and you will split the pot with someone playing a feeble A-2.

Someone with a nine is going to get involved. Unfortunately, they are beating you and you are playing just two outs against such a hand. The most likely result here is that you bet the flop and everyone folds. Not a bad result certainly, but if someone comes along with you then your hand is not that exciting.

3b)

The flop has completely missed you but, considering that it has, it is about as good as could be hoped for. It is quite likely that this raggedy collection missed everyone else too. You can still bet your hand confidently. If somebody has a four you are in big trouble, but even if an opponent has a seven or is playing a small pair, you still have six outs and a reasonable chance to make a better hand by the river.

3c)

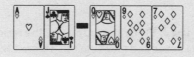

The flop has again completely missed you, and this time there is no good news. The flop is high-ish, moderately connected, and it is likely that one of the blinds has got a piece of this. The queen is bad news, as if an opponent has paired the queen then your only out is with an ace. The two-flush also hurts you. You don't even have the benefit of a gutshot draw to generate a few extra outs against a better hand. This is just a mess.

Betting concepts

Now we have some experience of assessing how our hand has connected with the flop, we need to consider how we will play the hand on the flop and beyond. To do this we need to bet our hand successfully.

The language of poker

Betting is the language of poker. Every time someone makes a bet (or indeed a check or a call) they are essentially saying something about their hand. Your job, as a poker player, is to interpret this language and act accordingly. However, this is not a universal language – everyone will speak a slightly different dialect. Weak players are generally easy to interpret. When a weak player makes a strong play (betting or raising) it generally means one of the following:

1) "I have a strong hand."
2) "I think my hand is the best right now."

When a tough player makes a strong play it can take on a much wider range of meanings. As well as...

1) "I have a strong hand."
2) "I think my hand is the best right now."

... he might also be saying...

3) "I want you to think I have a strong hand."
4) "I think you have a weak hand."
5) "I have very good chances to make the best hand."

or even...

6) "I am going to bully you. Are you going to stand up to me?"

However, before you can start to interpret your opponents' betting you need to be aware of the basic strategies for playing hands post-flop. These are: the free card, betting, raising and check-raising.

The free card

There may be no such thing as a free lunch, but free cards certainly exist, and they are a key component of poker. A free card is any card you get, either on the turn or river, for which you do not have to "pay" a bet. If you currently hold the better/best hand, then giving a free card is bad news – you are effectively giving your opponent(s) infinite pot odds. Conversely, if you are behind in a pot and receive a free card, this is very good news. You are now the happy punter in receipt of infinite pot odds.

The idea of a free card is closely tied in with the idea of "protection". If you hold what is currently the best hand and you bet (or raise), you force other players to pay to get to the river. By doing so, you are "protecting" your hand. If you do not bet/raise at appropriate moments, then your opponents will receive free/cheap cards and you will have failed to protect your hand.

> *TIP: Strong players absolutely loathe giving free cards and will do anything to avoid it. Weak players give them all over the place.*

It might seem strange to introduce the idea of a free card before discussing betting. However, in a sense, the purpose of most bets is to avoid giving free cards. Furthermore, as we shall see, sometimes you need to bet (or raise) in order to obtain free cards.

Betting

When you think you have the best hand, you should nearly always bet. This may seem blindingly obvious, but you would be surprised how many players, especially at low limits, are content to check and call with good hands and hope that their opponents will "bet their hands for them". Betting accomplishes various things that checking and calling simply can't:

Reasons to bet

1) If you do have the best hand you guarantee getting more money into the pot.

2) You avoid giving free cards. If your opponents have drawing hands you force them to pay to try and improve.

3) It is possible that everyone else will fold and you will win the pot at once. This is rarely a bad thing.

4) You obtain information about the opposition's hands. If you check, they bet and you call, you have no idea at all about their hands. They may just have bet because you showed weakness by checking. Then again, they may actually have a good hand. You can't be sure. However, if you bet and they call then they ought to have something. It may not be very much but if they had nothing at all, they would probably have folded.

Raising

As we know, when there has been a bet (and maybe one or more calls) and the play comes to you there is the option of raising. A raise is often made as a pure "value" play. You think you have the best hand, so you raise to get more money into the pot.

However, raising is also often used as a tactical device, especially on the flop. Before discussing when this can be a strong play, we need to consider the phenomenon of "checking to the raiser".

Checking to the raiser

A typical occurrence in low-limit games (this is much less the case in middle- and higher-limit games) is that players will "check to the raiser". This means that if a player shows strength on a previous round, players having to speak before this player on the subsequent round will "defer to the authority" of this player by checking.

Here is a typical situation where it can be good to make a tactical raise. Four players see the flop and you are on the button and will be last to speak. Note that you are thus in the best possible position. The first player bets, the next player folds and the third player calls. You have a reasonable hand which you want to play but you cannot be certain that your hand is best.

Now, you could call and see what arrives on the turn, but another play is to raise. Note that this is the flop round so the extra cost (compared to calling) is only one small bet. Now if both your opponents are compliant they will just call your raise (rather than re-raising) and then check to you when the turn card comes.

Now you are in a good position. If you do not like the look of the turn card then you can check and take a free card. Note that this is not, strictly speaking, a free card. You created the possibility of making this play with a raise on the flop. That cost you an extra small bet. However, you have now saved yourself one big bet, for a net gain of one small bet.

However, if the turn card looks promising (it may not necessarily have to help you for this to be the case – it may just appear likely that it has not helped your opponents), you have the option of betting.

By raising on the flop (and not being reraised) you have taken control of the hand and the other players are dancing to your tune.

Check-raising

A check-raise occurs when a player initially checks on the betting round and then subsequently raises in response to a bet. If you have a strong hand and you are in early position then this is a tactic well

worth considering. If you feel fairly sure that someone will bet –
allowing you to check-raise – then this is usually the best play. There
are two reasons for this:

Reasons to check-raise

1) You get extra money into the pot.

2) Anyone holding a drawing hand now has to call two bets instead
of one bet and thus their pot odds are much worse.

However, the drawback of attempting a check-raise is that no-one
may bet and you will have allowed the dreaded free card.

Pot odds (again)

When you are involved in a pot you will often (sadly enough) come to
the conclusion that you do not currently hold the best hand. If your
hand appears to be well beaten then you will fold. However, as we saw
in the preceding chapters, there are often quite good chances for
weaker hands to improve to winning hands by hitting their outs.
Whether you now have a profitable strategy of sticking around and
seeing if this will happen depend on the pot odds.

Now that we have considered the factors that affect post-flop play,
we need to move on to specific strategies as to how to play our hands.

Chapter 9

Post-flop strategy

The previous chapter was rather theoretical. Now let's look at some practical examples that demonstrate how these concepts are applied in actual hands. In all of these examples we will assume that you are playing in a $2-$4 game where the small is $1 and the big blind is $2.

In the following examples we will see all of the earlier ideas coming into play. We will follow the thought processes of a competent hold'em player as they decide what to do in various situations.

Hold'em is a complex game and there are hundreds of possible combinations of your hand, your opponents' hands, the board, the pre-flop play, the size of the pot etc. It is impossible to prepare for all eventualities. Hold'em is a game where experience counts a great deal. When you start playing you probably won't have much of a feel for what you are trying to do, unless you are a very natural, instinctive card player.

In this chapter I am going to give you a head start by demonstrating some basic plays and also by giving you an idea of the kinds of things you should be thinking about during a hand.

I am not going to provide specific guidelines such as: "if you flop top pair with a good kicker and there is a bet before you, you should do such and such," or "if you flop middle pair and it is checked to you, you should..." I don't think such advice is particularly helpful. Poker is highly situational and quite subtle factors can affect your decisions. What I am going to do is guide you through the kind of thought processes that a competent player would have that would affect their decisions.

When to raise

When one of your opponents has a good hand but you have a better one, you will want to put in a raise at some point. Where to do this is a tricky decision, but the following examples demonstrate the factors that should influence your decision.

Example 1

You are on the button with K♥-K♠ in an online game. A middle player limps and the cut-off calls. You raise, the big blind calls, as do the middle player and the cut-off. There is $17 in the pot and four players. The flop comes as follows:

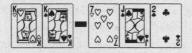

Your first job is to assess the flop. As we noted before, this is a great flop for you. Adopting the principle of checking to the raiser, everyone now checks and – obviously – you bet. The big blind folds but the middle player raises (actually check-raises) and the cut-off folds.

By raising, the middle player is suggesting that he thinks he has the best hand. So, is this likely? If you think about it you will quickly see that it is not. The hands that currently beat you are: A-A and J-J (not likely – he would have raised with these pre-flop), J-7, J-2 and 7-2 (these are very strange hands to play) 7-7 and 2-2 (these are possible). So the only realistic hands to worry about are 7-7 and 2-2. However, there are very many more hands that would look good to him that you are beating, eg A-J, K-J, Q-J, J-10, 8-7, 7-6, A-7, A-2 etc.

He has probably made a pair of jacks and thinks he has the best hand. From his point of view this is quite likely. You could easily have raised with something like 9-9, 10-10, A-K, A-Q or even K-Q, and all of these hands would now be losing to his.

You, however, know better. It is almost certain that you have the best hand here, and so you re-raise and your opponent calls. Both you and your opponent have contributed a further three small bets to the pot, adding $12. There is $29 in the pot and two players. The turn brings:

This is a harmless card, often referred to as a blank.

> **NOTE: A blank is a card which arrives on the turn or river and is most unlikely to be of help to any of the players in the pot.**

Your opponent checks and you bet. He calls. Note that the betting unit increases on this round to $4. Thus you have each contributed a further $4, bring the pot to $37. The river brings:

You bet once again and you opponent calls. Your kings take the pot which finally totals $45.

After the river betting was complete, your opponent called your bet and you showed your pair of kings (or rather the software did this for you automatically). In live play you would also have turned over your cards and then if your opponent was beaten (as he was here) he simply mucks his cards. The same thing happens online but with one crucial difference. On virtually all sites it possible to get a hand history which reveals the hole cards of all players who were involved in a showdown. You should always keep an eye on this as it is crucial to see what kind of hands your opponents are calling you with. In this particular example, the hand history shows that your opponent held J♦-10♥ for a pair of jacks.

Raising on the turn

This all seems rather straightforward and you took down a nice pot. However, there was, in fact, another way you could have played the hand. Let's consider the situation on the flop when the middle player raises you. You worked out that you almost certainly had the best hand and so re-raised, which was quite reasonable. However, there was another way to play the hand which would have been slightly more profitable. Instead of raising, you simply call. Now there is $25 in the pot.

When the turn card arrives it is very likely that your opponent will assume that he is winning and bet. Now you raise. Since your opponent holds top pair he will probably call, bringing the pot to $41. He will then call again when you bet the river and the final pot will be $49 which is $4 more than previously. By waiting until the turn to raise, you have made an extra $2.

This may not sound like much, but reeling in these extra bets is crucial in limit hold'em. One day you will be on the wrong side of this deal, but you will lose $2 less than your opponent did here. The luck will have balanced out, but your skilful play will be showing a $2 profit.

It is because of the possibility of plays such as these that I believe you have to consider flop and turn play together. The call on the flop does not make sense in isolation because you almost certainly have the best hand. However, it is part of a plan which involves raising on the turn.

Outs and pot odds

Much of the time it will be fairly obvious that you do not currently have the best hand in the pot. Perhaps you started with the best hand pre-flop but the flop has been a bad one for you. Or maybe you played a speculative hand that only connected slightly with the flop. In such cases a consideration of pot odds is crucial to assess whether continuing to play is a profitable proposition.

Example 2

You are on the button with K♥-K♠. A middle player limps and the cut-off calls. You raise, the big blind calls as do the middle player and the cut-off. There is $17 in the pot and four players. The flop comes as follows:

As we saw before this is a very dangerous flop for you. Nevertheless, everybody checks to you. Now you should bet. Even though the flop is scary you should not check – this is a very bad time to give a free card. After you bet the big blind then check-raises and the middle player calls. The cut-off folds. Now you can fold, call or raise. So, what do you do?

You should call. Folding is much too feeble. Although the board is scary, you do have an overpair and it is still quite likely that you have the best hand, though your opponents undoubtedly have a lot of outs against you. Re-raising is not a terrible play but in this particular situation it is over-aggressive. The key point here is that your call closes the betting. If you raise you keep the betting open and are then vulnerable to a further re-raise.

There are very many hands that the big blind could hold where he will be a big favourite over you and re-raise, eg Q-9, 9-7, J-J, 10-10, 8-8, J-10, J-8, 10-8. When we tried to think of hands that our opponent could have that were beating us in Example 1, we could come up with only 2-2 and 7-7 – nothing else made sense. Here, however, because the board is so coordinated, numerous hands are beating us.

> **TIP: When you are concerned that you may not have the best hand and your call will close the betting, this is often the best play.**

So, you call. There is $29 in the pot and three players. Now let's consider various different possibilities for the turn card.

Example 2a)

The big blind bets and the middle player calls. There is $37 in the pot. What do you do?

To answer this question we need to go through a quick deductive process.

1) Are we winning?

Most unlikely. We have two opponents and someone (most likely the big blind) probably has a nine. Even if no-one has a nine, someone will have two pair or even a set.

2) So, we will assume that we are not winning. Do we have outs to improve to a winning hand?

Yes, we do. An ace or a nine will complete a straight.

3) Are any of these outs tainted?

Possibly. The A♣ and the 9♣ will put three clubs on the board and the passive, calling play of the middle player suggests that he may be on a flush draw, although we cannot be certain.

4) Do we have pot odds to play?

Yes. There are 46 remaining cards and either six or eight are outs for us. Even if we assume the worst and allow ourselves just six outs, this gives us odds of 40-to-6 or about 7-to-1. The pot odds are 37-to-4 (we need to put $4 into a $37 pot) which is about 9-to-1. We can certainly call.

5) Is there anything else to worry about?

Yes. If someone has A-K, they have made the nut straight and we will need to hit an ace just to tie. However, this is highly improbable. If the big blind had A-K he would probably not have raised on the flop and if the middle player had A-K he would raise now rather than call.

6) Since we can call, is there any mileage in raising?

No. In principle, when you have decided that you can call it is always good to consider the possibility of raising, but here you will just get re-raised by a player holding a nine and end up with an unprofitable draw.

If you are new to the game of hold'em this may seem terribly complicated but it isn't really. I have deliberately broken the thought process down into numerous steps to clarify it. In reality an experienced player would take about two seconds to think: "There are four cards to a straight on board ... I'm probably losing ... looks like I could have eight outs ... $37 in the pot, $4 to call ... easy call."

It is rather like learning to drive. For a learner driver a simple task such as changing gears can seem immensely difficult. There are so many things to remember: ease off the accelerator, depress the clutch, select a gear, change gear, release the clutch, hand back on the steering wheel and so on. All the while there is all the other stuff to worry about: steering, looking in front of you, checking the rear-view mirror, watching for road signs, traffic lights etc. A total nightmare. Put like this it is a wonder anybody ever learns to drive. However, as with all repetitive tasks, after a while control of the car becomes easier and – eventually – it becomes second nature.

Now let's try another scenario.

Example 2b)

We have the same turn card but now after the big blind bets the middle player raises. There is $41 in the pot. What do you do? Well, let's ask the same questions:

1) Are we winning?

No way. The middle player surely has a nine even if the big blind doesn't.

2) So, we will assume that we are not winning. Do we have outs to improve to a winning hand?

Yes, we do. An ace or a nine will complete a straight.

3) Are any of these outs tainted?
Possibly. Someone may have two clubs for a flush draw. However, that doesn't seem all that likely.

4) Do we have pot odds to play?
Let's work it out. Let's be optimistic and assume that we do have eight outs. There are 46 remaining cards which gives us odds of 38-to-8 or about 5-to-1. The pot odds are 41-to-8 (we need to put $8 into a $41 pot) which is also about 5-to-1. So, if this is a valid calculation we have a borderline call.

5) Is there anything else to worry about?
Yes. There is a ton of other stuff to worry about. For a start it looks like there is at least one nine out against us which cuts our pot odds from 38-to-8 to 39-to-7 or possibly even 40-6. This is now pushing up towards 6-to-1 or 7-to-1. Since our call is borderline in the first place, this quickly makes it unprofitable.

Next, there is a danger that someone else has a king too. Then we will only split the pot if we do improve.

Finally, our call does not close the betting. If the big blind has a nine he will re-raise (and there may even be a subsequent cap from the middle player). Action like this will trash our pot odds.

6) So, what should we do?
Fold. Calling is far too risky.

Can you see what has happened here? By raising, the middle player has successfully protected his hand.

Playing a strong draw

In previous examples we have considered play when you had a modest drawing hand and were mainly interested in whether you had sufficient pot odds to compete. Sometimes you have a much stronger drawing hand and we will now look at ways to handle such holdings.

Example 3

An early player limps and it is passed round to you on the button. You hold A♣-J♣ and you raise. Both blinds fold and the early player calls. There is $11 in the pot and two players. The flop brings:

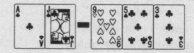

Just for a change I am going to reveal to you the hand held by the early player: he holds 10♦-9♦ and has made top pair. He is a decent, thinking player and he suspects that you might have a couple of high cards that have missed the flop (he is right), Rather than checking to the raiser and allowing you the possibility of a free card, he now bets. What do you do?

Let's look at some different ways to handle the situation:

1) Playing the draw

You obviously have a fine drawing hand with four cards to a flush and two overcards. Thus if the early player is winning you will have up to 15 outs (nine clubs, three aces and three jacks). There is $13 in the pot and it is $2 to call. I would hope that by now you do not even need to do the pot odds calculation – it is obvious that you must easily have value for a call. Therefore you call. There is $15 in the pot and two players. The turn brings:

This is a rather scary card for the early player as he is worried that you have a couple of high cards and this king may have enabled you to make a pair. Nevertheless, he is a good player and if he is winning, he does not want to give a free card, so he grits his teeth and bets. He is hoping that his fear that the king has helped you is unfounded. Of course he is worried that you are playing a hand such as A-K and will now raise, putting him in an awkward situation. However, the king has not helped you but you certainly have pot odds for your draw and so you call.

Finally the river arrives:

Oh dear. Your fine drawing hand has hit blanks. Your opponent again bets and you fold.

Well, that wasn't terribly successful – can we do any better?

2) The free card raise

If you have gone through the earlier material carefully, I would hope that you can spot a better play on the flop. You have position and so after the early player bets out you raise. The early player is now concerned that you might have a big pocket pair and so just calls.

The turn is again the K♥ which – from the early player's point of view – is rather ugly. He checks and, as the king has not helped you, you check it back, taking your free card. As we know, unfortunately you miss your draw. However, this is at least an improvement over the previous play in that now your flop raise has saved you one small bet and, although you lose the pot, you end up $2 better off.

Nevertheless I would hope that you still find this all slightly unsatisfactory. You had a wonderful drawing hand. Couldn't you somehow have put a bit more pressure on your opponent? Indeed you could...

3) The semi-bluff

The semi-bluff is a powerful poker play and you must have it in your armoury. A semi-bluff is an extension of the concept of bluffing.

Everyone who has ever been exposed to poker is familiar with the idea of a bluff. In fact, if you ask some people about poker they will suggest that it is a game where the main area of skill is deciding whether your opponent is bluffing or not. Having looked through the material in this book, I would hope that by now you appreciate that poker is a rather more subtle game than this. Nevertheless, everyone knows what a bluff is. A bluff is basically a lie. You don't have a hand but you bet strongly. Your hope is that the opposition will be intimidated by your strong play and will fold. This is the only point of your play.

The semi-bluff is a more sophisticated weapon. It is a strong play made with a drawing hand. It is still basically a bluff, but now you have two ways to win:

How a semi-bluff works

1) Your opponent might believe you and fold.

2) You might complete your draw and win anyway.

On the above hand there are two ways to employ the semi-bluff: the "normal" way and the aggressive way. Let's consider them in turn.

3a) A normal semi-bluff

The flop play of the hand is identical to the play in the "free card raise" scenario. You raise and the early player just calls. Now the K♥ comes down in the turn.

As we noted before, this is a scary card for the early player (who is holding 10♦-9♦) and he checks. In the free card scenario, you checked it back and took your free card. However, a better play is to bet.

Now the early player has a difficult decision. You have shown a great deal of strength in this hand: you raised pre-flop, you raised on the flop and you bet the turn. In fact, you don't actually have anything at all, but it looks like you must have a good hand. His bet on the flop implied that he had made a pair, but you fired straight back with a raise and then bet the turn. Surely, he will think (assuming, of course, that he thinks at all – always a dangerous assumption), you must have a big pair to play so aggressively?

At this point there is $23 in the pot and it costs him $4 to call. If you really do have a higher pair then he is playing just five outs and he does not have pot odds to call (work it out). If he thinks it through, it will be difficult for him to call here.

However, many poker players are stubborn and he may well call, suspicious that you might be bluffing and (from his point of view) having a few outs anyway. Now you have 15 outs on the river and still have a 2-to-1 chance to make the best hand anyway.

Your raise and follow up bet is a very powerful play:

1) You give him a tough decision on the turn.

2) You have a decent chance to win the hand anyway.

All in all, a classic semi-bluff.

However, there is an even more powerful way to play:

3b) An aggressive semi-bluff

This time, when the early player bets the flop you simply call. Now when the K♥ arrives and he bets, you raise. You have now mimicked the play in Example 1 ("When to raise"), when you had a big overpair and waited for the turn to pull the trigger. With a bit of luck this will scare the pants off him and he will fold. Even if he doesn't then, again, you have your 15 outs and a 2-to-1 chance to win anyway.

Which is best?

There are pros and cons to both plays. On the whole – against an average player – I would favour the line in 3a. You put him under pressure when he has committed slightly less money to the pot, and weaker players find it easier to release hands before they get too deeply involved. Stronger players are different and against a tough player I would opt for 3b. Tough players are less impressed with raises on the cheap street but have more respect for a raise on the expensive street. They are also more capable of giving up on a hand when they are already in deep – weaker players will usually want to see it through (often more out of curiosity than anything else), whatever the cost.

WARNING: The semi-bluff is a great play and is a powerful weapon that enables you to maximise the potential of drawing hands. However, it is more successful against better players who are capable of folding. In low-level games it should be used with caution as players in these games are often very reluctant to fold no matter how bad the situation looks.

Conditions for a successful semi-bluff

1) As few opponents as possible, preferably just one. Even two is really too many.

2) It looks as if your opponent probably has a modest holding.

3) It helps if a scare card has just appeared.

4) You have a decent number of outs if you get called.

5) Your opponent appears to be a decent player who can fold a hand.

River play

When you get to see the river card no further improvement to your hand is possible. The river is a tense moment. Sometimes you have had the best hand all along but maybe one or more opponents have been playing drawing hands against you. You are naturally concerned that their drawing hands might have got there and your hand may no longer be best.

Some players are capable of taking the initiative and playing hands very aggressively on the flop and turn but then freeze up when the river comes. Some vaguely scary card lands on the board and they are worried that if they bet, they will get raised and then feel obliged to call. Not only will they suffer the pain of losing a big pot but they will have tossed away an extra bet on the river to boot. So they freeze. They check and their opponent checks the hand back. It turns out they were winning but their opponent had a good enough hand to call. By freezing up, they have thrown away a bet.

Mind you, they probably won't care, or even realise that they have made a mistake. They will just be happy that their hand has stood up and they have taken down the pot. This is a bad attitude.

> *TIP: A major element of the skill in limit hold'em is about squeezing the maximum possible profit from your winning hands. Failing to pick up easy bets on the river is a bad error.*

Occasionally, it is fairly obvious that your hand may no longer be good and a check is in order. However, whenever you have position over your opponent and they have already checked then you should almost always bet. If they really had made a good hand they might well have bet, being concerned that you might simply check behind them. It takes experience to be able to judge these situations well, but here are some examples.

Example 4

You are on the button with J♠-J♦. A middle players opens with a raise and you re-raise. Everyone folds and the middle player calls. You see the flop heads up and it arrives.

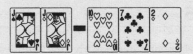

This is a very good flop – no overcards. Your opponent checks, you bet and he calls. The turn is a blank – the 4♠ and again the play goes check, bet and he calls. The river is the K♠ and your opponent checks.

Now the weak player thinks: "Oh dear. An overcard. Maybe he has A-K or even K-Q and has outdrawn by making a pair. I'd better play safe and check." So he checks, his opponent shows 9♠-9♣ and our safety-first expert has thrown away a bet.

Checking the river here is way too feeble. Sure, he might have a king but:

1) There are a load of other hands he might be calling with, eg A-Q, A-J, Q-10, J-10, 10-9 or any smallish pair etc. Some players, especially at the low limits will call you down with any old rubbish.

2) If he really did have a king he might well have bet the river himself.

> *WARNING: An important part of poker is trying to read your opponents' hands and decide what sort of cards they might be playing. This is not the same as forever fearing the worst and assuming that any remotely scary card that arrives is bound to help them. Poker is not a game for pessimists.*

Basic principle for betting the river

If, on the balance of probabilities, you are winning, and you can get called by a worse hand, then bet.

This principle certainly applied in Example 4. Here is another example.

Example 5

A middle player limps and you raise from the button with A♠-10♠. The blinds fold and the middle player calls. You see the flop heads up and it comes down.

Your opponent now bets. You have a fine draw with a four-flush and an overcard and make the good play of raising. The middle player calls. The turn is the 2♦, he checks and now you prefer to bet rather than take the free card. He calls. This is the situation:

Now if the river is a complete blank and your opponent checks, you should check behind him and hope that your hand is good. It probably isn't, but if he can beat ace high he will certainly call, so betting accomplishes nothing. However, if the river is the 10♦, then you should bet. It is quite possible that he has a hand such as 8-8, 9-9, an even smaller pair, or that he has a hand with a seven. He will probably call with all of these. It is possible that he has a jack, but with top pair in a heads-up situation he may well have played more aggressively than he actually did. A bet here should have positive expectation, which is the key factor. Thus, if on three occasions he calls and you win, whilst on one occasion he calls and turns up with a jack, then you have made money with the bet.

Bridge

by **Sally Brock**

Chapter 1

Before we begin

Before you can hope to learn how to play bridge it is important that you understand about tricks and trumps.

Trick-taking

The concept of a trick occurs in many card games, with whist perhaps being the most common.

Sit at a table with at least one other person. For the purposes of this description, let us assume there are three of you. Shuffle the deck and deal out three cards to each player. Let us say each player has the following cards:

A	B	C
nine of diamonds	queen of diamonds	three of hearts
five of clubs	five of diamonds	six of clubs
eight of diamonds	queen of hearts	queen of spades

Player A, the one to the left of the dealer, starts by placing a card, say the nine of diamonds on the table. Now it is Player B's turn. He must play a diamond if he has one. Suppose he plays the queen of diamonds. As it is higher than the nine he is "winning the trick". Now it is Player C's turn. As he doesn't have a diamond he must "discard".

He would usually discard his lowest card, here the three of hearts. Player B has won the trick. B gathers these three cards together and places them face down in front of him.

Because Player B has won the trick it is his turn to lead to the next trick. Suppose he plays the queen of hearts. Player C is out of hearts so discards the six of clubs. Player A is also out of hearts so he discards the five of clubs. Player B has again won the trick.

To the third trick he leads his remaining card, the five of diamonds. Player C is still out of diamonds so must discard the queen of spades. Player A wins the trick with the eight of diamonds. Note that even though the queen of spades is the highest card it does not win the trick because it is not in the same suit as the one led.

Repeat this exercise a few times until you get the hang of it.

A trick always contains the same number of cards as there are players in the game (four at bridge). It is important to remember that you must follow suit if you can. Failure to do so is called a revoke and is against the rules of most trick-taking games, including bridge.

Playing with a trump suit

A trump suit is a suit that is selected in some way to be superior to the other three suits. In some games this selection is made by cutting the deck, in others it is made by one player choosing the trump suit that affects his hand to best advantage; in bridge the selection of the trump suit is a complicated process called bidding which we will discuss later.

When there is a trump suit, every card in that suit is superior to every card in all the other suits. But again, you must follow suit if you can. Let us look at the play of three tricks with a trump suit:

A	B	C
five of diamonds	ace of clubs	four of hearts
ace of hearts	three of diamonds	four of clubs
ten of diamonds	five of spades	king of diamonds

First suppose diamonds were trumps. Suppose Player A is on lead and chooses the ace of hearts. Player B, who has no hearts, trumps in with the three of diamonds. Player C has to follow suit with the four of hearts. Player B wins the trick and then leads the ace of clubs. Player C follows with the four of clubs and Player A trumps with the five of diamonds. Player A's last card is the ten of diamonds. Player B contributes the five of spades and Player C wins the trick with the king of diamonds.

Now suppose clubs are trumps. Again Player A leads the ace of hearts. Player B has no hearts and may play whatever he likes. Since his ace of clubs will make a trick whenever he plays it there may be tactical reasons for withholding it, but for the sake of argument let us say he does choose to trump with it.

Player C follows with the four of hearts. Player B now leads the three of diamonds. Player C plays the king of diamonds and Player A the five of diamonds. It is Player C's trick. Player C now plays his last card, the four of clubs. As it is the only trump out he will win the trick even though it is the lowest card.

Again, deal out three cards again and try this exercise a few times until you are happy with it.

Bridge is a partnership game

Bridge is a game for four people and it uses all the deck. So each player begins with thirteen cards. There are thirteen tricks with four cards in each trick. To make for ease of explanation, the four people playing are referred to as North, South, East and West. North and South are partners, as are their opponents, East and West. As you would expect, West sits on South's left, while East sits on South's right.

As it is a partnership game, each side must try to make the most of its combined assets. Generally speaking, if East is last to play and West is winning the trick, then East will play a low card, letting West win the trick. With no trumps involved, if North plays a king to a trick, then South would not play his ace to that trick. South is quite happy for North to win the trick.

When a bridge hand is printed in a book or a magazine, it usually has a square in the middle, with the letters N, S, W and E in it, to help you identify the positions:

Chapter 2

Starting with minibridge

The game of bridge is made up of two parts: the bidding and the play. First there is the bidding, or auction, at the end of which it is decided which partnership is attempting to make how many tricks with what, if any, trump suit. After the bidding comes the actual play of the hand.

Declarer and dummy

This person in the hot seat at the end of the auction is known as the declarer. Let us suppose the bidding results in South becoming declarer and attempting to make ten tricks with spades as trumps. West, the player on South's left, makes his opening lead and then North, South's partner, puts all his cards on the table, leaving South in control of those thirteen cards as well as the thirteen cards in his own hand. This player, North here, who takes no further part in proceeding, is known as the dummy.

Why play minibridge?

Classical methods of teaching bridge used to involve starting with the bidding, because that is what happens first at the table. The trouble with that approach is that a lot of bidding theory needs to be learnt before a final contract can be reached and the play begin, and that can be boring for students of the game.

A few years ago a new game was invented which has had a huge impact on the teaching of bridge. It dispenses with the bidding altogether so you can get started on the play of the hand. Bidding theory can then be interspersed with the play of the hand which is much more interesting for learners. This new basic form of bridge is called minibridge and is what we are going to start with in this book.

Basic minibridge

Four players sit around a table. One of them becomes dealer. In "correct" circles the dealer is selected by cutting the deck. Each player in turn takes a few cards off the top of the deck, then faces the bottom card. The one with the highest card becomes the dealer. The whole deck is dealt out, with thirteen cards to each player. The players each look at their cards.

Counting points

The first thing to be done is for each player to count their high-card points. This is a simple method of hand evaluation and will be useful when you move on to bridge proper.

$$
\begin{array}{rcl}
\text{an ace} & = & 4 \text{ points} \\
\text{a king} & = & 3 \text{ points} \\
\text{a queen} & = & 2 \text{ points} \\
\text{a jack} & = & 1 \text{ point}
\end{array}
$$

Announcing points

Now each player in turn, starting with the dealer and moving clockwise around the table, announces how many points they hold. There are 10 points in each suit (4+3+2+1) and 40 in the whole deck, so these totals should add up to 40. When you are starting out, they may not do so, in which case you ask everyone to check and try again.

Deciding who is declarer

The two partnerships now add their points together and the side with the higher total becomes the declaring side (if they both add up to 20, then redeal and start again). The player on the declaring side who has the higher total becomes declarer (if they are the same then the one who was first to speak becomes declarer).

What next?

Now for an example hand. With all the examples, it is advised that you deal out the cards according to the diagram and play it through as you read. Let us suppose the following hand is dealt by South:

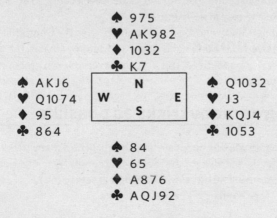

South announces 11 points, West 10 points, North 10 points and East 9 points. North/South have 21 and East/West 19, so North/South become the declaring side. Since South had one more point than North, South becomes declarer.

Note that if West had had 12 points and East 7, then South would still be declarer, even though he had fewer points than West.

Putting down the dummy

The next thing in minibridge is for the dummy to lay his cards down on the table, with each suit laid out in an overlapping vertical column in descending order. (In bridge proper the opening lead is made before the dummy goes down.)

Choosing trumps

When South sees the dummy he must decide whether to play in a trump suit or without trumps (no-trumps). A simple rule to start with is to choose to play with a trump suit if you have a combined suit holding of eight or more cards; with two such holdings, then choose the longer, and if you have two of the same length then choose the stronger.

Here the longest combined holding is just seven cards, so South should choose to play in no-trumps.

Note that had South chosen a suit contract, then the trump suit should be moved to the left-hand side of the dummy (that is, the left from declarer's perspective). This is so that everyone remembers what are trumps.

Making as many tricks as possible

A bit later on we will talk about setting targets of how many tricks to try for, but for the moment both sides should simply try to make as many tricks as possible by using their side's assets to the full.
Let us repeat the hand from the previous page.

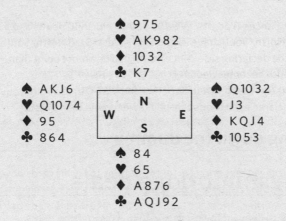

♠ 975
♥ A K 9 8 2
♦ 1 0 3 2
♣ K 7

♠ A K J 6
♥ Q 1 0 7 4
♦ 9 5
♣ 8 6 4

♠ Q 1 0 3 2
♥ J 3
♦ K Q J 4
♣ 1 0 5 3

♠ 8 4
♥ 6 5
♦ A 8 7 6
♣ A Q J 9 2

NOTE: One of the most attractive suits to lead is one where a strong honour (picture card) combination is held.

Here West should start with the ace of spades. In a no-trump contract he knows this will win the trick. At trick two he continues with the king of spades and this also wins the trick. He then plays a low spade and trick three is won by East's queen. When declarer discards a diamond (he discards from a suit in which he has no hope of taking any tricks), East knows West has the jack of spades and could play a fourth round of the suit. However, East has a strong diamond combination and can see that if he can dislodge declarer's ace then he will be able to take at least two more diamond tricks. If East plays the fourth round of spades immediately, West may not know to play a diamond next, so East, who does know, must play a diamond.

NOTE: It is a good rule in any card game to take control and direct the play when you know what to do but your partner may not.

South wins the ace of diamonds and needs to set about taking some of his tricks. There are five club tricks for the taking provided declarer is careful. If he starts by playing the ace of clubs and then a club to dummy's king he will have blocked the suit. Although the queen, jack and nine in his hand will be winners, he has no entry with which to reach them. He must broach the suit by playing a club to dummy's king, and then a club to his ace, followed by the queen, jack and nine of clubs.

> **NOTE: When cashing tricks in a suit, you should generally play the honours from the shorter holding first.**

After his five club tricks he can also make the ace and king of hearts, but then will lose the last two tricks to East/West. All in all, declarer makes eight tricks and the defenders five.

Some minibridge deals

Remember to deal out the cards and follow through the play.

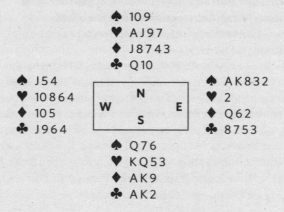

```
                   ♠ 10 9
                   ♥ A J 9 7
                   ♦ J 8 7 4 3
                   ♣ Q 10
    ♠ J 5 4                          ♠ A K 8 3 2
    ♥ 10 8 6 4        N              ♥ 2
    ♦ 10 5       W         E         ♦ Q 6 2
    ♣ J 9 6 4        S              ♣ 8 7 5 3
                   ♠ Q 7 6
                   ♥ K Q 5 3
                   ♦ A K 9
                   ♣ A K 2
```

> **NOTE: It is a convention in bridge writing to make South declarer on all hands. Of course, in real life South is declarer on only about a quarter of the deals, but it is easier to follow if all the deals are viewed from the same perspective.**

Suppose North is the dealer. He announces 8 points, East has 9, South has the grand total of 21 and West a paltry 2. So South becomes declarer. When he sees dummy he notices that he has eight-card fits in both hearts and diamonds. The stronger suit is hearts, where he has the ace, king, queen and jack between the two hands, so that is what he settles on as trumps.

West has no attractive honour holding to lead from this time. However, he knows his partner has some values and he can see that dummy is weak in spades, so a low spade is a reasonable choice.

East wins the king of spades, and then plays the ace of spades followed, for want of anything better, by a third round of the suit which declarer wins with the queen.

> **NOTE: When you are declarer in a trump contract, one of the main issues you must address is when to draw trumps. On the one hand, you do not want to allow your opponents to make any small trumps by trumping (or ruffing) your winners. But, on the other hand, one of the main reasons for choosing to play in a trump contract is so that you can make extra winners by ruffing, in which case it could be a mistake to play too many trumps too soon.**

Here there is no obvious ruffing to do, so you should simply draw four rounds of trumps. Then play your club winners – the queen first (to avoid blocking the suit), followed by the ace and king. Then play the ace and king of diamonds. When the queen does not drop in two rounds you concede the last trick to East, and make ten tricks in total.

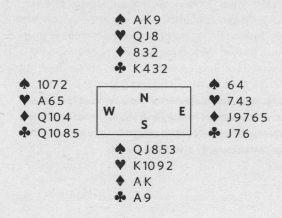

West, the dealer, announces his 8 points first, then North his 13, East 2 and South 17. South becomes declarer and with eight spades between the two hands chooses that suit as trumps.

> *NOTE: When choosing an opening lead against a suit contract it is generally a good idea to avoid suits with unsupported aces.*

With no obvious opening lead, West starts with a low club. There is no ruffing to be done in dummy so declarer should draw trumps immediately. This means he needs to play three rounds of spades.

> *NOTE: Counting is an important aspect of bridge. If you have eight trumps between your two hands, that means the opponents have five. About two-thirds of the time they will divide three and two which means you need to play three rounds of the suit in order to draw all the opponents' trumps.*

Having drawn trumps, declarer is left with six top winners: two long trumps in his hand, the ace and king of clubs and the ace and king of diamonds. If he plays out all those winners, that is all he will make. At the end he will play the king of hearts which West will win.

Provided West has been paying attention and discarded his low hearts on the spades, he will be able to take the rest of the tricks in the minor suits.

There is a better plan for declarer, though. Although he has no top tricks in hearts, he can establish three tricks in the suit once the ace is knocked out. Before playing any more trumps or clubs or diamonds, he should play a heart. West can win his ace but has no winners to cash. Whatever he returns, declarer wins and makes the remainder of the tricks.

> *NOTE: Suit establishment is an important concept. When you have sequential honour cards you may need to play one of them to knock out a higher card in order to promote the trick-taking capacity of your lower cards.*

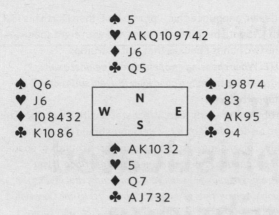

♠ 5
♥ A K Q 10 9 7 4 2
♦ J 6
♣ Q 5

♠ Q 6
♥ J 6
♦ 10 8 4 3 2
♣ K 10 8 6

♠ J 9 8 7 4
♥ 8 3
♦ A K 9 5
♣ 9 4

♠ A K 10 3 2
♥ 5
♦ Q 7
♣ A J 7 3 2

A more distributional deal this time. More often than not the suits are distributed fairly evenly between the four hands, but sometimes one hand has a disproportionately large or small number of a suit. These hands can be exciting as sometimes you can make a lot of tricks with a relatively small number of high-card points.

Here South announces 14 points, West 6, North 12 and East 8. South becomes declarer. Looking at just his hand, South was not expecting to choose hearts as trumps, but when he sees the strong eight-card suit in the dummy, it is clear that hearts must be trumps.

With no particularly attractive suit to lead from, West chooses a diamond and East wins the king and the ace. It does not look as if there is much chance of any further tricks in that suit, so at trick three East plays the nine of clubs. Declarer should win his ace of clubs and draw the opponents' trumps. Here it takes two rounds, but if you're not sure you can often, as here, afford an extra round. Then play the ace and king of spades, discarding dummy's queen of clubs. Now all dummy's cards are trumps, and winners. South makes eleven tricks.

Note that this is the first time it has really mattered that we chose a trump suit rather than to play in no-trumps. In the previous two deals, though we chose to play in a suit contract, we would have made the same number of tricks in no-trumps. Here if we had chosen no-trumps, East/West would have taken the first five diamond tricks.

Chapter 3

More sophisticated minibridge

Setting targets

The time has come to set yourselves some targets. It is all very well to try to make as many tricks as possible, but sometimes your combined point count is only 21 while on other occasions it may be well into the thirties. Here is a sensible schedule:

Points	Number of tricks
21–22	7
23–24	8
25–26	9
27–28	10
29–32	11
33–36	12
37+	13

You will notice quite quickly that these targets work better when your hands are fairly balanced, ie don't have very long suits or singletons or voids. You may find that when you have a very good "fit", ie the combined length of your longest suit is say ten cards or more, that you don't need so many high-card points to take the requisite number of tricks.

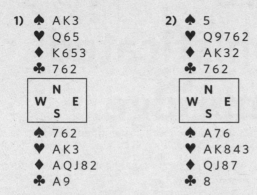

1)
♠ A K 3
♥ Q 6 5
♦ K 6 5 3
♣ 7 6 2

    N
W   E
    S

♠ 7 6 2
♥ A K 3
♦ A Q J 8 2
♣ A 9

2)
♠ 5
♥ Q 9 7 6 2
♦ A K 3 2
♣ 7 6 2

    N
W   E
    S

♠ A 7 6
♥ A K 8 4 3
♦ Q J 8 7
♣ 8

On Hand **1)**, you have 30 combined points. If you count your winners (two in spades, three in hearts, four in diamonds and one in clubs) you will find there are eleven, just as there should be.

On Hand **2)**, though, it is a different matter. You have 23 points, which gives you a target of eight tricks. Even if you were never to ruff in either hand you would make ten tricks (one spade, five hearts and four diamonds). Good technique (see Ruffing, which we will cover later in this chapter) should lead to twelve.

More on choosing a suit

In the last chapter I gave simple guidance about whether or not to choose a suit or no-trumps: go for the suit contract when you have an eight-card fit or better. But a guideline should not be an excuse for not using your brain and there are plenty of exceptions...

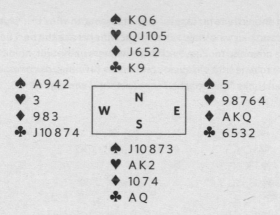

```
                    ♠ KQ6
                    ♥ QJ105
                    ♦ J652
                    ♣ K9
  ♠ A942                          ♠ 5
  ♥ 3              N              ♥ 98764
  ♦ 983         W     E          ♦ AKQ
  ♣ J10874         S             ♣ 6532
                    ♠ J10873
                    ♥ AK2
                    ♦ 1074
                    ♣ AQ
```

South = 14 points, West = 5, North = 12, East = 9.

South becomes declarer, and with 26 points between the two hands his target is to make nine tricks.

Under our previous rules South would choose spades as trumps, but look what happens.

West leads the three of hearts won by South with the ace (win with the shorter holding, remember). South plays a trump. West wins his ace and plays a diamond which East wins with the queen.

> **NOTE: When winning a trick as a defender, you should always play the lowest of touching honours. When that wins the trick partner will be able to place you with the higher cards as well.**

East plays a heart back which West ruffs. West leads another diamond and receives another heart ruff. West leads another diamond and East tries another heart, but declarer ruffs high, draws West's last trump and makes the remainder. South made only seven tricks and is two short of his target.

Now suppose that when South looks at the dummy he sees that he has no need to ruff anything. He has two stoppers in his shortest suit, clubs, and needs to knock out only one card, the ace of spades, before he has more than sufficient tricks for his target. Let us see what happens when he choose to play in no-trumps.

West should lead his longest suit, clubs. South wins in his hand with the ace and plays a spade. When West wins his ace the best he can do is play a diamond for East to cash his winners in the suit, holding declarer to nine tricks. If West continues with clubs, declarer will make ten tricks (four spades, four hearts and two clubs).

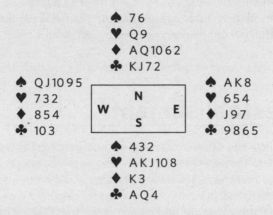

South = 17 points, West = 3, North = 12, East = 8.

South becomes declarer, and with 29 points between the two hands his target is eleven tricks. Under our old rules he has no eight-card fit and would choose to play in no-trumps. West would lead the queen of spades. Perhaps East would play low on this trick and West would continue with a second spade. East would take his ace and king and declarer would fall one short of his target.

However, East can do even better of course. The same principles apply in defence as they do in declarer play. Had East been declarer, he would have seen the necessity of winning the first spade in the shorter hand and would have played the king on the first round of the suit. He should do the same when defending. He knows that West will have the jack of spades to go with his queen (or he would have led his fourth highest, not an honour). He can also see that if West has only 3 points, then he cannot have an entry outside spades. If order to take as many tricks as possible, East should overtake his partner's queen of spades with the king, cash the ace of spades and continue with a spade to West's jack. Then declarer will make only eight tricks, three short of his target.

Now suppose declarer thinks clearly when he sees the dummy and notices the spade weakness. Suppose he chooses hearts to be trumps. Now when the defenders start with three rounds of spades declarer can ruff the third round in the dummy. Then he draws the trumps and has plenty of winners to make the rest of the tricks.

I am now going to move on to look at techniques of good cardplay.

Suit establishment

There is a difference between "cashing" winners and "establishing" winners. When you have top tricks, ie the ace and perhaps the king, then when you play them, you are cashing them; you know they will hold the trick (unless, in a suit contract, someone ruffs). But if you are missing the ace and have just the king and queen, then they are not winners as of right – they must be "established". To do this you play the king which forces someone to play the ace; then your queen becomes a winner. Here is a simple example of suit establishment.

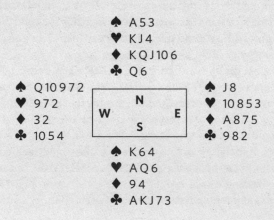

South = 17 points, West = 2, North = 16, East = 5.

South becomes declarer and, with no eight-card fit and no obvious weakness, chooses no-trumps. With 33 points between the two hands, South's target is twelve tricks. West leads the ten of spades.

A vital part of cardplay which we have barely mentioned so far is counting. It is often said that the only mathematical skills needed to be a good bridge player is the ability to count up to thirteen. I wouldn't go quite as far as that – counting up to 40 since there are 40 points in the deck can come in handy too. But counting is the key to the correct play on so many hands.

NOTE: Get into the habit of counting: counting winners, counting losers, and counting points.

Declarer can see that he has two spade tricks, three hearts and four (probably five) club tricks, so needs three more for his contract. If he simply cashes all those tricks, when he eventually plays a diamond, the defenders will have winners to make in hearts and spades. However, if instead he concentrates on 'establishing tricks', and plays a diamond, East will win and there is nothing damaging for him to do. Declarer then has plenty of winners – fourteen, in fact, although of course he has lost one!

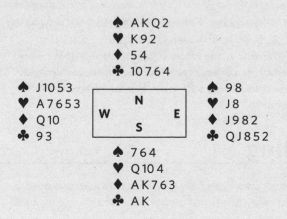

```
              ♠ A K Q 2
              ♥ K 9 2
              ♦ 5 4
              ♣ 10 7 6 4
  ♠ J 10 5 3              ♠ 9 8
  ♥ A 7 6 5 3     N       ♥ J 8
  ♦ Q 10       W     E    ♦ J 9 8 2
  ♣ 9 3           S       ♣ Q J 8 5 2
              ♠ 7 6 4
              ♥ Q 10 4
              ♦ A K 7 6 3
              ♣ A K
```

South = 16 points, West = 7, North = 12, East = 5.

South becomes declarer and chooses to play in no-trumps. With 28 points between the two hands, his target is ten tricks. West leads the five of hearts, fourth highest of his longest and strongest (see Chapter 4 for more about opening leads).

Declarer counts his tricks: three (maybe four) spade tricks, two heart tricks on the lead, two diamonds and two clubs – nine in total unless spades break. His best chance of establishing more tricks lies in diamonds. Provided neither opponent holds more than four diamonds, declarer can establish an extra trick there.

Declarer plays low from dummy at trick one and wins East's jack with his queen. He then plays the ace and king of diamonds and another diamond, losing the lead to East. East has nothing better to do than continue hearts. West wins the ace of hearts and plays another which is won by dummy's king. Declarer now crosses to his hand with the ace of clubs and plays another diamond. He knows it is safe to do this because East has the last diamond (West has shown out) and he is known not to have any more hearts to play. East would probably play a club. Declarer, who has already discarded two clubs from the dummy, wins and cashes his long diamond, discarding dummy's low spade. Now he has ten tricks whether spades break or not.

Of course, had someone discarded on the second (or first) top diamond, declarer would have had to try the spades.

> **NOTE: In no-trump contracts in particular, whether you are declarer or a defender you should look at establishing your small cards in long suits as well as establishing your honours.**

Ruffing

Thus far, the cardplay techniques we have studied have been concerned only with no-trump contracts, but a trump suit adds another element.

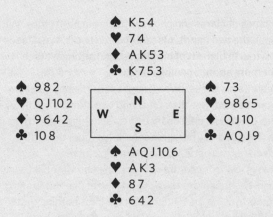

South = 14 points, West = 3, North = 13, East = 10.

South becomes declarer and chooses spades as trumps. With 27 points in the combined hands, his target is ten tricks. West leads the queen of hearts.

Declarer counts his tricks: five spades, two hearts, two diamonds and perhaps a club. Whether or not declarer can make a trick with the king of clubs depends on who has the ace. If West has the ace, declarer can lead a low club from his hand; if West plays the ace then the king is promoted, while if West plays low then the king wins the trick immediately. If East has the ace he will not play it unless the king is played from dummy so the king will not score a trick. Here, in minibridge – but not in bridge proper– declarer knows perfectly well that the East must have the ace because West has only 3 points.

So declarer needs to generate an extra trick, and the easiest way to do that is to ruff a heart in the dummy. Declarer wins the opening lead with his king of hearts and cashes just one round of trumps in his hand (he needs two trumps in dummy – one to take the ruff and one to enable him to get back to his hand to draw trumps).

When both opponents follow, he cashes the ace of hearts, and ruffs a heart in the dummy with the king of spades – it would be silly to ruff low and find that East could overruff. Then he plays a trump back to his hand and cashes the rest of trumps followed by the ace and king of diamonds to come to ten tricks.

Had either opponent shown out on the first round of trumps, declarer would not have had the luxury of being able to ruff a heart high in the dummy for that would have promoted a trump trick for the defence.

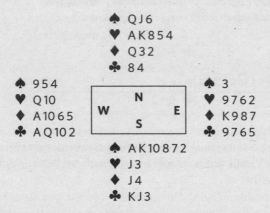

♠ Q J 6
♥ A K 8 5 4
♦ Q 3 2
♣ 8 4

♠ 9 5 4
♥ Q 10
♦ A 10 6 5
♣ A Q 10 2

♠ 3
♥ 9 7 6 2
♦ K 9 8 7
♣ 9 7 6 5

♠ A K 10 8 7 2
♥ J 3
♦ J 4
♣ K J 3

South = 13 points, West = 12, North = 12, East = 3.

South becomes declarer and chooses to play in spades. With a combined total of 25 points, his target is nine tricks.

West has an unattractive hand to lead from, especially as he knows that his partner has little in the way of help. He hits on the excellent lead of a trump.

On counting his tricks, declarer finds he has eight: six spades and two hearts. On a non-trump lead declarer could have more or less guaranteed his contract by playing on clubs, ruffing the third round in the dummy. However, if West started with both club honours, as indeed he did, and continues trumps whenever he gets the lead, he will scupper that plan.

The alternative is to establish dummy's heart suit. Declarer wins the trump lead cheaply and cashes the ace and king of hearts. Then he ruffs a heart high in his hand. Had the suit broken 3-3 he would have made an overtrick, but as it is he must now play a low spade to dummy's jack and ruff another heart high. Then he plays a low spade to dummy's queen, drawing West's last trump in the process. He then cashes dummy's long heart discarding a loser from his hand. He has thus made nine tricks, whatever the lie of the cards in the minors.

> *NOTE: Sometimes in a suit contract one of the two hands has a side suit that can be established by ruffing. This should be given priority over drawing trumps.*

The finesse

Earlier we saw a situation where declarer's ability to make a trick with the king of clubs depended on which opponent held the ace. This idea of a possible but not certain trick is very important in declarer play. There are many different situations with a similar concept. Consider these two positions:

1) A Q J

   4 3 2

2) A 3 2

   Q J 10

In both of these suit combinations you have two certain tricks by establishing a second winner in the way we have seen earlier. You cash the ace and then play the queen. An opponent wins his king and then your jack becomes a winner. But here you may be able to do better. If in **1)** you lead small from the South hand and play the jack (or queen) when West plays low, when West holds the king your jack will win the trick. You then cross back to your hand and play the suit again. If West plays low you play the queen which will hold the trick. When you cash your ace you will have made three tricks in the suit.

Of course, if East held the king he would win it when you played the jack on the first round and you would make only two tricks. But by taking the finesse you give yourself a roughly 50 per cent chance of making an extra trick.

Similarly, with **2)**, at trick one you lead the queen. If West has the king he has no winning play. If he plays the king you win the ace and your jack and ten become winners. If he plays low, so do you, and then you play the jack, and again he is in the same no-win position. As in **1)**, if East has the king he will win it on the first round, but again you had an even-money shot at an extra trick.

3) A Q 2

5 4 3

4) K Q 2

5 4 3

With **3)** you have one certain trick, but if West has the king, a 50 per cent chance, you can make an extra trick. When you lead low from the South hand, West has no winning play. If East has the king you just have the one trick you started with. The situation in **4)** is slightly different for it is the ace you are missing, not the king. Again, you have one certain trick by playing out the king which will establish the queen. But by leading towards the two honours you will make an extra trick whenever West has the ace.

Enough theory – time for some more hands!

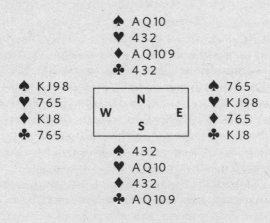

South = 12 points, West = 8, North = 12, East = 8.

South becomes declarer and chooses to play in no-trumps. With a combined total of 24 points, the target is eight tricks. West leads the eight of spades.

Declarer plays dummy's ten which holds the trick. He then plays a club to his nine which holds, a diamond to dummy's nine which holds, a club to the jack and queen, a diamond to the jack and queen, etc, etc. He is spoilt for choice and has more than thirteen tricks to take.

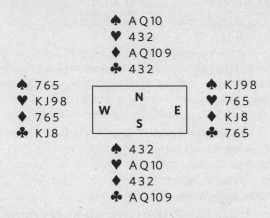

♠ A Q 10
♥ 4 3 2
♦ A Q 10 9
♣ 4 3 2

♠ 7 6 5
♥ K J 9 8
♦ 7 6 5
♣ K J 8

♠ K J 9 8
♥ 7 6 5
♦ K J 8
♣ 7 6 5

♠ 4 3 2
♥ A Q 10
♦ 4 3 2
♣ A Q 10 9

South = 12 points, West = 8, North = 12, East = 8.

South again becomes declarer and again chooses to play in no-trumps. With a combined total of 24 points, the target is again eight tricks. This time suppose West leads the seven of spades.

Declarer plays dummy's ten which loses to the jack. East switches to the seven of hearts and declarer's ten loses to the jack. Another spade sees the queen lose to East's king and another heart finesse loses to West's king... And so it goes on. This time declarer makes only his four aces – a nine-trick difference between this hand and the previous one where the North/South cards were identical.

This shows you the best and the worst that can happen; thankfully real life is usually a little different.

Scoring and the concept of game

So far the targets we have set for ourselves have been arbitrary, ie there has been no decision or judgement about how many tricks declarer was trying to make. In bridge proper the bidding decides the final contract (or target) and we need to take a look at how bridge is scored.

For every trick beyond six bid for and made you score:

1) If a minor suit (clubs or diamonds) is trumps: 20 points.
2) If a major suit (hearts or spades) is trumps: 30 points.
3) If there are no trumps: 40 points for the first trick and 30 points for each subsequent trick.

There is a bonus for bidding and making a contract that scores 100 points. Therefore you should try hard to bid to:
1) FIVE of a minor (5 x 20 = 100),
2) FOUR of a major (4 x 30 = 120)
3) or THREE no-trumps (40 + 30 + 30 = 100).
This contract that scores 100 (or more) points is called a game contract. If game has been announced before the play of the cards, and it is achieved, the declaring side gains a bonus of 300 points. If a partscore (ie one that scores less than 100) has been announced and achieved, the declaring side gains a bonus of 50 points.

On the other hand, if the declaring side does not reach its target, it does not score any points for the tricks it has achieved, rather the defending side gets 50 points each for every trick that the declaring side is short of its target.

In bridge proper there are further bonuses for bidding and making twelve tricks (a small slam) or thirteen tricks (a grand slam).

There is plenty more to be said on the subject of scoring at bridge but this is all you need to know at minibridge, for now we are going to allow you to choose your final contract.

Previously the target was set by simple arithmetic but now as well as deciding on your trump suit (or no-trumps), you also have to decide whether to go for partscore (seven tricks), game (nine tricks in no-trumps, ten tricks in a major or eleven tricks in a minor) or slam.

> **NOTE: Whether you are playing bridge or minibridge, you should try to bid and make a game contract whenever possible.**

Let's revisit an earlier hand to see how it would have worked out.

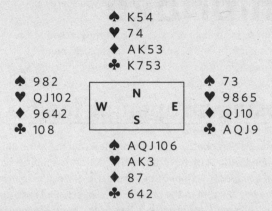

                    ♠ K54
                    ♥ 74
                    ♦ AK53
                    ♣ K753

    ♠ 982   ♠ 73
    ♥ QJ102   N   ♥ 9865
    ♦ 9642   W   E   ♦ QJ10
    ♣ 108   S   ♣ AQJ9

                    ♠ AQJ106
                    ♥ AK3
                    ♦ 87
                    ♣ 642

South is declarer and with eight spades between the two hands it is easy to choose them as trumps (see page 23). He can see that he has nine tricks on top (five spades, two hearts and two diamonds). All he needs to do is ruff a heart in the dummy to bring his total to ten. So he should choose to play in game with spades as trumps.

Chapter 4

Defending at minibridge

Choosing an opening lead

The principles behind choosing an opening lead are the same in bridge and minibridge, but in getting to the final contract different information is available. In minibridge there is precise information regarding the point-count of the other three players, while at bridge proper, the point-count information is less exact, but there may be more clues about everyone's distribution.

There are two factors you should take into account when selecting your opening lead:

1) The information you have about the opponents' hands: the number and location of their high-card points and whatever you can deduce about their distribution. It is generally better to lead through their strong holdings.

2) What you can see in your own hand. If you have three touching honours, for example, it is rarely wrong to lead the top one.

Active or passive?

The most important decision to be made is whether to go for an active or passive lead.

An active opening lead is akin to an ace at tennis. It aims to beat the contract (or at least set up tricks) in one fell swoop. However, in tennis if the ace fails it is likely to result in a fault and the pressure of a mediocre second service. In bridge, if the active lead fails it may result in giving away the contract with no hope of recovery.

A passive opening lead is like an underarm serve at tennis which simply seeks to put the ball into play. A passive lead seeks to give nothing away and let declarer make his own mistakes.

There are several reasons why you would choose one approach over the other:

1) When you think your opponents have bid conservatively and have plenty of values to spare you should go for an active lead. If you don't do something dramatic they would probably succeed in any event.

At minibridge you know how many points they have between them and how many tricks they have contracted for. If they are aiming for fewer tricks than they should according to the target table at the start of the previous chapter, then you should generally make an active lead. But if they are going for more tricks than their point-count would suggest you should tend to be more passive.

2) We have seen how differently the cards can lie for declarer. Sometimes they lie very well and sometimes very badly. In real life things are rarely as extreme as in that pair of hands, but if you see kings in dummy over your ace-queens or ace-queens in dummy over your kings, then the cards are lying well for declarer. On the other hand if there are small cards in dummy in the suits in which you hold honours and high cards in suits where you don't hold honours, then the cards are lying well for you and badly for declarer. When the cards are lying well for declarer you should be active; when they are lying badly for him you should be passive.

Here are a few examples:

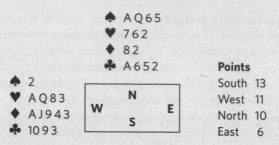

♠ A Q 6 5
♥ 7 6 2
♦ 8 2
♣ A 6 5 2

♠ 2
♥ A Q 8 3
♦ A J 9 4 3
♣ 10 9 3

Points
South 13
West 11
North 10
East 6

Suppose that South decides to try for game in spades. You know that this is a bit of a stretch because North/South have only 23 combined points. In addition, you know that the cards are not lying well for him. Any honours he has in the red suits will lose to yours; if he is missing any spade honours they will be with partner, over dummy's holding and there is no friendly trump break for him either. You want to make as passive an opening lead as possible.

That rules out the red suits. Unfortunately you have no idea how many trumps he has. If he has five or more, a trump would be passive and therefore an attractive shot. However, it is quite possible that he has only four trumps, in which case it could make life easy for declarer if your partner's trumps were, say, K-10-x-x. The best choice is a club. This cannot do anything for declarer that he could not do for himself.

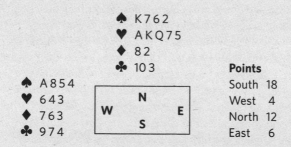

♠ K 7 6 2
♥ A K Q 7 5
♦ 8 2
♣ 10 3

♠ A 8 5 4
♥ 6 4 3
♦ 7 6 3
♣ 9 7 4

Points
South 18
West 4
North 12
East 6

Suppose South has opted for game in hearts. With a combined 30 points he has plenty to spare. In addition, your cards are not badly placed for him: your ace is in front of his king and any minor-suit honours your partner has will be well placed for declarer. Your best hope is to find partner with queen doubleton of spades and a minor-suit ace. Lead a low spade. With any luck declarer will play low from dummy. Your partner will win the queen and lead one back to your ace. Now a spade ruff and the minor-suit ace will mean one down.

> **NOTE: If you think declarer may go down in his contract, either because he has overstretched or the cards lie badly for him, then make a passive lead and hope to avoid helping him. However, if you think he is in a comfortable contract and the cards lie well for him, he will surely succeed unless you can find a chink in his armour via an active lead.**

Leading against no-trumps

It usually works best to lead from long suits against no-trump contracts. Even if you do not strike gold immediately, you may set up your long cards as winners. Suppose this is the layout:

```
                    A Q
     1 0 9 6 4 3 2  ┌─────────┐   8 7 5
                    └─────────┘
                    K J
```

Even though North/South hold all the honours, if you lead this suit at trick one and continue when you next get the lead, you will have knocked out all their stoppers. If either of you gain the lead again you will have four winners to take.

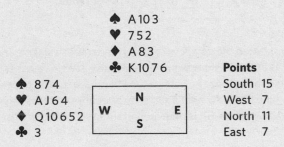

♠ A 10 3
♥ 7 5 2
♦ A 8 3
♣ K 10 7 6

♠ 8 7 4
♥ A J 6 4
♦ Q 10 6 5 2
♣ 3

| | W | N | E | S |
| | | | | |

Points

South	15
West	7
North	11
East	7

If South tries for game in no-trumps, lead the five of diamonds, fourth highest of your longest suit. Your best chance of establishing five tricks is to find partner with the king of diamonds. You will be able to knock out dummy's ace and cash the suit when you get in with the ace of hearts.

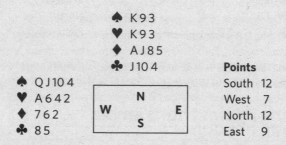

	♠ K93	
	♥ K93	
	♦ AJ85	
	♣ J10 4	

		Points	
♠ QJ10 4		South	12
♥ A642	N	West	7
♦ 762	W E	North	12
♣ 85	S	East	9

With two four-card suits you should look at your middle cards to help you decide. Here spades is a better choice, despite your having only 3 points in that suit as opposed to 4 points in hearts. If you can set up a couple of tricks in spades, your ace of hearts may be your entry to cash them.

Leading against a suit contract

Let's look again at the combination we saw earlier:

```
                    A Q
   10 9 6 4 3 2  [        ]  8 7 5
                    K J
```

Had you started the defence the same way against a suit contract, your efforts at establishing winners would have been in vain. Yes, you knocked out their stoppers, but this time they have trumps to deal with your long cards. Against a suit contract, considerations of length are less important; here it is more important to set up high cards.

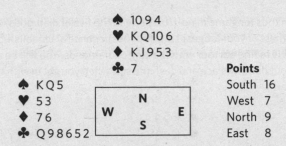

```
                ♠ 1094
                ♥ KQ106
                ♦ KJ953
                ♣ 7                    Points
  ♠ KQ5        ┌──────────┐            South  16
  ♥ 53         │     N    │            West   7
  ♦ 76         │ W      E │            North  9
  ♣ Q98652     │     S    │            East   8
               └──────────┘
```

If South opts to play in hearts, be it partscore or game, you should lead a top spade. In suit contracts it is important to take or set up your winners before declarer discards his losers on another suit.

Leading honours

Three touching honours make a most attractive opening lead – would that we were dealt such a holding on every hand. Against a suit contract this is almost always the best choice, though against no-trumps you should prefer your longest suit unless dummy is very strong in that department.

Two touching honours is also attractive but can be dangerous. Look at these two layouts:

```
1)        K104                2)        J65
    QJ6 ┌──────┐ 9832            KQ4 ┌──────┐ 10832
        └──────┘                     └──────┘
         A75                          A97
```

On layout **1)** West started with one sure trick, but if he leads the queen South wins with the ace and can later lead towards his king-ten, finessing West's jack. On layout **2)** West started with two tricks, but if he leads the king South will win his ace and later lead towards dummy's jack. In each case by leading the suit West loses a trick.

Although such a lead is more dangerous than leading from three honours, it can work well because it needs just one honour card from partner to succeed.

Against no-trumps, where you are more concerned with setting up long tricks than honours, if you are leading from a long suit containing two touching honours, it is usually better to lead a small card.

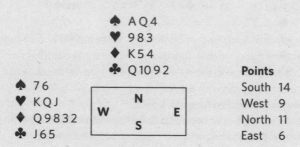

♠ A Q 4
♥ 9 8 3
♦ K 5 4
♣ Q 10 9 2

♠ 7 6
♥ K Q J
♦ Q 9 8 3 2
♣ J 6 5

Points
South 14
West 9
North 11
East 6

If South chooses to play in no-trumps, lead a low diamond. But if South chooses a suit contract, lead the king of hearts.

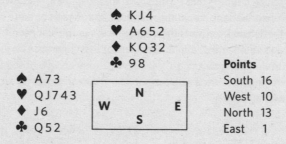

♠ K J 4
♥ A 6 5 2
♦ K Q 3 2
♣ 9 8

♠ A 7 3
♥ Q J 7 4 3
♦ J 6
♣ Q 5 2

Points
South 16
West 10
North 13
East 1

Against a suit contract, lead the queen of hearts, but against no-trumps it is better to lead a low card in the suit because your spot cards are very small.

Leading small cards

There is a convention in leading that is common worldwide: lead high spot cards from poor suits (ie suits containing no honours) and lead low spot cards when leading from honours. In the old days, people used to lead top of nothing when they held no honours, but nowadays it is more common to lead second from poor suits. This enables the leader to tell his partner how many cards he holds in the suit.

1) 9 7̲ 5 4 3   **2)** 9 7̲ 5 4   **3)** 9 7̲ 5   **4)** 9̲ 7

In each case lead the card underlined. With both **1)** and **2)** continue with the four, your original fourth highest (more about this later). With **3)** continue with the nine – by following upwards you make it clear that you began with a three-card holding. With **4)**, or any other doubleton, you should lead the top card.

When leading from honour cards the most common convention is to lead fourth highest (though you will find quite a few tournament players who prefer third and fifth). So...

1) Q 7 5 4̲ 3   **2)** Q 7 5 4̲   **3)** Q 7 5̲   **4)** Q 7

In each case lead the card underlined. On **1)** you will continue with the three, which will tell partner you began with a five-card (or longer) suit. On **2)** and **3)** partner may be able to tell immediately that you hold no more than four cards because he may be able to see the lower cards in his own hand or the dummy. Otherwise, when you follow upwards to the second round he will realise you cannot have a long suit. However, he will not be able to tell whether you have led from three or four cards and this ambiguity is why some people prefer third and fifth (when you lead lowest from an odd number and third highest from an even number).

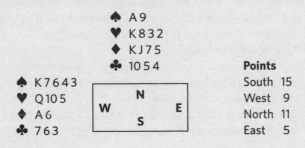

	Points	
	South	15
	West	9
	North	11
	East	5

Against a no-trump contract lead the four of spades, your fourth highest. Were South to choose to play in hearts it is a harder choice: lead either the four of spades or a club.

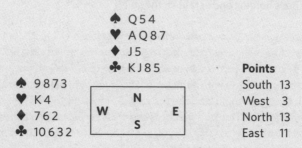

	♠ Q 5 4		
	♥ A Q 8 7		
	♦ J 5		
	♣ K J 8 5	**Points**	
♠ 9 8 7 3		South	13
♥ K 4	N	West	3
♦ 7 6 2	W E	North	13
♣ 1 0 6 3 2	S	East	11

As dummy's clubs are quite strong, a spade looks best, against either no-trumps or a suit contract. Choose the eight to show a poor holding.

Leading singletons against suit contracts

Many people like to lead singletons against suit contracts. After all, if they find their partner with the ace they can score a ruff straight away. However, this can be a two-edged sword because your aim is rarely to take just two defensive tricks and you must keep your eye on the larger target. Very often your short suit is declarer's side suit (ie his main source of tricks outside trumps). By leading it for him you have helped him set up winners rather than set up winners for your own side. In addition, of course, you might have helped him pick up partner's holding – maybe partner would have made two tricks had you not led the suit but your lead has reduced him to one.
DON'T lead a singleton when...

1) You have a strong trump holding – when you have trump tricks declarer needs to draw them at some stage and you will only make his life easier if you ruff with them.

2) When you have most of your side's assets – if your partner does not hold many high cards the chances of finding him with the ace of the suit you lead are small – and even if you do you will not be able to put him again to get a second ruff.

3) You know it is declarer's suit – you will only help him pick up partner's holding and establish the suit.

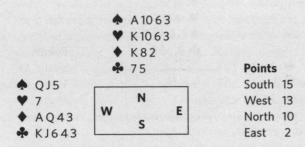

	Points	
	South	15
	West	13
	North	10
	East	2

It would be foolish to lead your singleton against a spade contract as all it might do is pick up partner's queen of hearts. Your best shot here is the ace of diamonds and then another diamond.

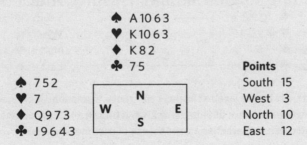

	Points	
	South	15
	West	3
	North	10
	East	12

Here, with such a weak hand, a singleton heart lead is advised against a spade contract. If partner has the ace of hearts he can give you a ruff. Then if he has another ace you can get a second ruff.

Leading trumps

A trump lead can work well. Your opponents have probably chosen to play with a trump suit because they want to do some ruffing. By leading a trump you can cut down their ability to do this. Also, people generally choose strong suits to be trumps so a trump lead can be a good passive choice. However, if declarer's trump holding has some holes in it, a trump lead may be all he needs to pick up your trumps for minimum loss.

It is generally better to lead a trump from length rather than shortage. When you are the defender with the trump length you know whether you have small cards (making it a good passive choice), or a couple of honours (when it is better to let declarer play the suit himself). When you have the shorter holding you do not know this so there is more risk attached.

You should generally avoid a trump lead if you think declarer has a good side suit that may run for him.

```
              ♠ K74
              ♥ 82
              ♦ AQ53
              ♣ 7643
                                    Points
  ♠ 10982    ┌───────────┐         South  15
  ♥ KJ94     │     N     │         West   10
  ♦ 76       │  W     E  │         North   9
  ♣ AQ10     │     S     │         East    6
              └───────────┘
```

In this example, against a spade contract a trump lead looks good for several reason: it avoids giving away a trick in another suit and it is unlikely that declarer has a good source of tricks in a side suit.

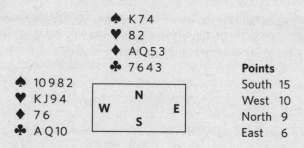

```
              ♠ K74
              ♥ 82
              ♦ AQJ53
              ♣ 764
                                    Points
  ♠ 10982    ┌───────────┐         South  14
  ♥ KJ94     │     N     │         West   10
  ♦ 76       │  W     E  │         North  10
  ♣ AQ10     │     S     │         East    6
              └───────────┘
```

Here, again against a spade contract, with the strength of dummy's diamond suit increased there is too much danger that if a spade is led, declarer will be able to draw trumps and run diamonds, discarding his losers. East/West's best bet is to take four tricks in hearts and clubs (or one in diamonds and three in hearts and clubs). To this end a heart is the best shot. If this runs round to declarer's ace-queen there is still a chance of taking a diamond and three clubs with partner's 6 points.

Helping partner in defence

There are two main aspects to defence at bridge and minibridge:
1) Finding out about the hand; and
2) Working out what to do with the information.

In order for both defenders to find out about the hand they must exchange information about the cards that they hold. I should stress that this information must be exchanged legally. At both games your behaviour should be exemplary. You should not indicate from your words or manner that you either like or dislike any of partner's actions, either in defence or, in bridge proper, in the bidding.

Playing the lower of touching honours

Suppose this is the layout of a suit:

```
              876
  K932     [        ]     QJ5
              A104
```

You are East and your partner leads the two. You should play the jack, not the queen. If you play the jack and declarer wins with the ace, partner will know that you have the queen, for if declarer held both the ace and the queen he would have won with the queen. If you play the queen you deny the jack and when partner gets the lead again he will know that he needs to put you in to lead through declarer's jack.

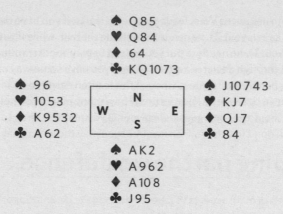

South = 16 points, West = 7, North = 9, East = 8.

South opts for game in no-trumps. West leads the three of diamonds, East plays the jack and declarer wins with the ace. Declarer continues with the jack of clubs which West wins with the ace. West now knows that his partner holds the queen of diamonds for if declarer had held the ace and queen he would have won with the queen. So West continues with another low diamond and the defenders take four winners in the suit.

Encouraging a continuation

Whether partner has led an honour card or a small card he needs to know if he is on the right track or if he needs to direct his attention elsewhere. It is your job to do your best to help him. Generally speaking, you play a high card to tell him you like the suit, and a small card to tell him to try something else (though you may meet players in the tournament world who prefer to do this the other way around).

Look at these two layouts:

1)			2)		
	876				876	
AKJ2		1093		AKJ2		Q93
	Q54				1054	

In both instances West leads the ace of hearts. If you have the queen, as in layout **2)**, he needs to continue the suit, while if you don't, as in layout **1)**, he needs to put you on lead to play another round of the suit through declarer's queen. Unless you have some way of helping him he has to guess (though this is often easier to do in minibridge because he knows exactly how many points you hold).

This should not be a guess. On layout **1)** you play the three to say that you don't like the suit; on layout **2)** you play the nine to say that you do.

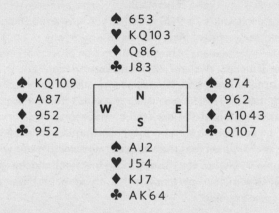

```
                        ♠ 6 5 3
                        ♥ K Q 10 3
                        ♦ Q 8 6
                        ♣ J 8 3
        ♠ K Q 10 9                       ♠ 8 7 4
        ♥ A 8 7          N               ♥ 9 6 2
        ♦ 9 5 2      W       E           ♦ A 10 4 3
        ♣ 9 5 2          S               ♣ Q 10 7
                        ♠ A J 2
                        ♥ J 5 4
                        ♦ K J 7
                        ♣ A K 6 4
```

South = 17 points, West = 9, North = 8, East = 6.

Declarer chooses to try for game in no-trumps. West starts with the king of spades. If declarer wins the ace and plays a heart West can win his ace but then he has a problem. Where is the jack of spades? If East has it the suit can be cashed, but if declarer has it West must try to put his partner in. East should play a low spade at trick one with no honour in the suit; if he held the jack (or ace) he should play his highest spot card.

An expert declarer in the South seat would duck the king of spades lead at trick one. Now an unwary West may continue spades and give declarer a second trick in the suit. Again, a signal from East is vital.

When declarer plays a suit

When declarer plays a suit it is not necessary to tell partner whether or not you like the suit. It usually becomes apparent very quickly. However, it can be useful to tell partner how many cards you have in the suit. Even more important than knowing the location of the other high cards is trying to work out the distribution of everyone's hands.

The most common convention is to play a high card followed by a low card (known as an echo or peter) when you have an even number, and a low card followed by a high card when you have an odd number (though, some tournament players do this the other way around).

We will see later that one of the most important aspects of card play (either defence or declarer play) concerns communications. The two partnership hands (either the defenders or declarer and dummy) need to maintain the links between their two hands. There is no point in one hand having lots of winners if there is no entry to those winners. Conversely, it is good play to try to disrupt your opponents' communications. Sometimes the way to do this is not to take your winners immediately, but you can only judge the best time to take your winners if you know how many cards everyone has in the suit. Here is a simple example:

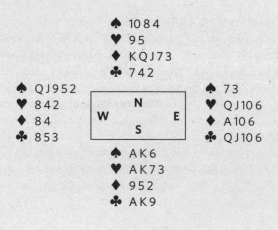

South = 21 points, West = 3, North = 6, East = 10.

South chooses to try for game in no-trumps. West leads the queen of spades which declarer wins with the king. He continues with a diamond to dummy's king. If East wins this trick and continues spades declarer will make ten tricks (six top tricks in his hand and four diamonds in the dummy). But look at the effect of East ducking (ie refusing to win) the king of diamonds, and then the queen of diamonds. Now declarer can make only two diamond tricks and will go one down.

Some basic rules of defence

Second hand plays low

A general rule of defence is that if you are second to play (ie declarer is leading to the trick, either himself or from dummy), then you should play low.

Look at this layout:

1)	K 10 3		**2)**	K 10 3	
J 8 4		Q 6 2	J 8 4		A 6 2
	A 9 7 5			Q 9 7 5	

In both instances declarer leads low from his hand towards the dummy. If you play the jack he will win the king and then, on layout **1)**, can lead towards his ace-nine, picking up the suit without loss. There is no need for you to play the jack. If you play low your side is guaranteed one trick in the suit.

If the layout is as in **2)**, South needs to guess which defender holds the jack and if you play your jack you remove that guess. If you play low he may well play the king, in which case you would later make a trick with your jack.

Third hand plays high

Conversely, if you are the third hand to play, ie your partner has led to the trick, then you should play high.

Again, look at a couple of layouts:

1) 765   **2)** K76
K942 ☐ Q103   A942 ☐ Q103
AJ8   J85

When partner leads the two you must play your queen. On layout **1)** it will force out declarer's ace and when you next get in you can lead through his jack-eight and your partner's king and nine will both score tricks. If instead you play the ten, declarer will make his jack.
On layout **2)**, if you play the queen and return the suit, declarer will just make the king. On the other hand, if you wrongly play the ten he will make his jack at trick one and his king later on when the suit is next played.

When dummy has an honour

bridge is not a game which can be reduced to a set of simple rules. These guideline are no substitute for thought. Look at these two layouts from East's point of view:

1) J65   **2)** J76
K942 ☐ Q103   Q942 ☐ K103
A87   A85

On layout **1)**, with the jack in dummy your queen and ten are more or less equals. Here, of course, if declarer plays low from dummy you play your ten, knowing that it will force just as high an honour as the queen would. Note that if you were to play your queen declarer would make a second trick in the suit by leading towards dummy's jack.

Layout **2)** is harder. If partner has the ace and queen it does not matter whether you play the king or ten when declarer plays low from dummy. If partner has the queen and declarer the ace, the ten is necessary to stop declarer making a second trick with dummy's jack. But what if partner has the ace and declarer the queen? The answer to this is that once partner has led the suit, declarer, if he has the queen, will always make one trick in the suit. So you might as well let him make the first trick rather than a trick later on. Once your ten has forced his queen, you will be able to take three tricks in the suit (against no-trumps) whenever your side gains the lead.

Cover an honour with an honour

Although we have seen that a basic rule of defence is that second hand should play low, this is only when declarer leads low. When declarer (or dummy) leads an honour it is a different matter. Look at these layouts:

1)	Q 6 5		**2)**	Q J 5	
10 7 2	☐	K 4 3	10 7 2	☐	K 4 3
	A J 9 8			A 9 8 6	

Declarer leads the queen from dummy. On layout **1)** you must play your king. Then, ultimately, partner will make a trick with his ten. If instead you play low, declarer will play a second round towards his ace-jack and bring in the whole suit for no loser.

On layout **2)** when declarer plays the queen you must not play your king. If you do, declarer will be able to run the nine on the next round and pick up your partner's ten. What you need to do is cover on the second round, when declarer plays the jack. That way your side is still guaranteed its one trick in the suit.

This may sound very confusing but the rule is: when declarer plays an honour from dummy, cover unless you can see that there is a supporting honour left in the dummy.

Chapter 5

The uncontested auction

The time has come to move on to bridge proper and to start learning about bidding. So far we have been able to see partner's hand (ie the dummy) before deciding on the final contract. Now we have to exchange sufficient information to make that decision without seeing any cards other than our own.

Bidding is like a conversation in a foreign language. You need to agree with your partner what language you are speaking and make sure that your vocabulary is up to it. After that you take it in turns to speak until a conclusion is reached.

As in minibridge, the auction has to establish both the denomination and the target, in terms of the number of tricks declarer is aiming to make. A series of calls are made by each player in turn. The calls we shall consider at the moment are bids and pass (later on we shall also look at double and redouble). As in a real-life auction, each bid has to be higher than the previous one. Here is an example auction:

West	North	East	South
1♣	1♥	Pass	2♥
3♣	Pass	Pass	Pass

The number part of a bid refers to the number of tricks you contract to make above six. As there are thirteen tricks in the deck, if you are going to make more than your share you must make more than six. The denomination part of the bid refers to what trumps are going to be.

West opened the bidding with one club. This means he will try to make seven tricks with clubs as trumps. Because hearts are higher ranking than clubs (the order of the suits in ascending order is clubs, diamonds, hearts, spades, no-trumps) North can bid hearts without raising the level, so he bids one heart. East has nothing to say so passes. South has some support for hearts and a few high cards, so raises to two hearts, aiming to make eight tricks. If West wishes to bid again, he can bid at the two level in spades or no-trumps only, because they are the only two denominations higher than hearts. If he wishes to bid clubs or diamonds (or hearts) he must bid at the three level. Three clubs contracts to make nine tricks with clubs as trumps. The other three players have nothing to say and the auction ends, as do all auctions, with three passes.

As in minibridge there are bonuses for making game (nine tricks in no-trumps, ten tricks in hearts or spades, eleven tricks in clubs or diamonds), so enterprise and optimism is rewarded. On the other hand, if you contract for more tricks than you can make, your opponents will score instead of you.

Scoring and vulnerability

Before we move on to look at bidding we need to have a further look at scoring at bridge.

Rubber bridge is usually played in people's homes where just four people are gathered together. The word rubber refers to a period of play which is made up of the best of three games. As in minibridge, in order to make a game you need to make nine tricks in no-trumps, ten tricks in hearts or spades or eleven tricks in clubs or diamonds.

Game does not have to be bid in one go. If you bid and make two hearts, say, on the first deal (60 points), and then three clubs on the next (another 60 points), your total is over 100. You have scored a game. However, if your opponents bid a game on the second deal your first 60 points are wiped out and you have to start again.

When one side has made a game they become vulnerable. When you are vulnerable you are halfway to winning the rubber. The rewards are greater, but so are the penalties if you fail.

If you win a two-game rubber you score 500 points, while if you win a three-game rubber you score 300 points.

Undertricks, ie the tricks you are short of your contract, score 50 points non-vulnerable and 100 points vulnerable.

If you bid and make a small slam (12 tricks) you score a bonus of 500 points non-vulnerable or 750 points vulnerable in addition to the game bonus. If you bid and make a grand slam (13 tricks) you score a bonus of 1,000 non-vulnerable and 1,500 vulnerable, again in addition to the game bonus.

At rubber bridge honours also count. If you have four of the top five honours in trumps score 100 points; if you have all five or all four aces in a no-trump contract score 150 points.

Doubles and redoubles

A further complication is that any contract may be doubled. Effectively, a defender states that they do not think declarer will succeed in his contract and wishes to double the stakes. If declarer is still certain that he will succeed he can redouble, further raising the stakes.

If you make a doubled contract, the points you score for making your tricks are doubled, you score an extra 50 points "for the insult", and if the double takes you up to game, then you score a game bonus as well. So if you were doubled in two hearts and made it you would score 60 x 2 for your eight tricks, 50 for the insult, plus a game bonus of 300 non-vulnerable or 500 vulnerable because you are now deemed to have made four hearts. The total would be 470 non-vulnerable and 670 vulnerable.

However, the consequences of failure are worse. Non-vulnerable, instead of losing 50 points you lose 100 for the first trick, 200 for the next two and 300 thereafter. So, three down is 500, and four down 800. Vulnerable, you lose 200 for the first trick and 300 thereafter.

A redouble doubles everything again, whether you succeed of fail, including the insult which goes up to 100.

A rubber bridge score pad

Here is a typical rubber bridge score pad:

WE	THEY
	300
800	750
100	200
30	50
60	120
40	
60	
	180

Deal 1: We bid two hearts and made it with an overtrick (60 "below the line" for bidding two hearts, ie it scores towards game, and 30 "above the line").

Deal 2: Our opponents bid two spades, we doubled it but it made (120 below the line and 50 above for the insult). So they had made a game and a line was drawn under the scores.

Deal 3: Our opponents bid four spades but it went one down so we scored 100 above the line.

Deal 4: We bid one no-trump and made it for 40 below the line.

Deal 5: We bid three clubs and made it for 60 points, thus making 100 points in total and game for us, so again a line was drawn.

Deal 6: We bid four hearts but the opponents bid on to four spades. We doubled them and it went three down for 800 to us.

Deal 7: They bid and made six hearts: 180 points below the line and a 750 bonus for a vulnerable small slam. This won the rubber for them, being their second game, so they scored 300 for a three-game rubber.

So in total we lost the rubber by 510 points (1,600–1,090).

Basic hand evaluation

Although minibridge does not have bidding in the same way as bridge proper, some of the things we have already learned will come in very useful here.

1) Counting points. You are already used to counting points when you pick up your hand, and that is what you should do at bridge too.
2) Targets. In minibridge we saw that it takes roughly 3 points to make one trick (there are 40 points in the deck and thirteen tricks). This is the same in bridge. So, in order to contract to make more tricks than your share, you need more points than average. Generally speaking you need 12 points to open the bidding (2 points more than average to make half a trick more than average).
3) Distribution. In minibridge we saw that when you had long suits and/or plenty of trumps between the two hands then you could make many more tricks than your point-count would suggest. This is also true in bridge. A general guideline is that if you have a six-card suit or two five-card suits, then you can open the bidding with 11 points, or even 10 if all your points are in your long suits or you have even more extreme distribution.

The following hands all qualify as opening bids:

1)	♠ A K 4	2)	♠ 5	3)	♠ A K 8 7 2
	♥ Q J 8		♥ A K 6 5 3 2		♥ 7
	♦ Q 10 5 2		♦ A 6 5		♦ K 10 8 6 2
	♣ 9 8 2		♣ 8 7 2		♣ 8 7

Hand **1)** has 12 high-card points. Hand **2)** has only 11 but the six-card heart suit is good compensation. On Hand **3)** the total has dropped to 10 but the two good five-card suits are worth a lot in terms of trick-taking potential.
Sometimes, of course, you have more points, ie a stronger hand:

4)	♠ A K 4	5)	♠ 5	6)	♠ A K Q 7 2
	♥ Q J 8		♥ A K Q 5 3 2		♥ 7
	♦ A Q 5		♦ A K 5		♦ A K 10 6 2
	♣ K 9 8 2		♣ Q 7 2		♣ 8 7

These hands are all very strong. After partner has responded you will have to take strong action to show your extra values.

What to open

When you have a five-card or longer suit, there is no problem. You simply open one of your long suit. Don't worry too much about the quality of your suit: when choosing a trump suit, it is length not strength that is important.

1)	♠ A K 6 5 3	2)	♠ A 4	3)	♠ 6
	♥ A 6 5		♥ 6 5 4 3 2		♥ A 5
	♦ Q 7		♦ A K Q		♦ K Q J 2
	♣ 8 7 2		♣ 10 5 4		♣ A Q 8 5 4 2

On Hand **1)** open one spade. On Hand **2)** open one heart despite having such a weak five-card suit. On Hand **3)** open one club.

Should you be lucky enough to hold two five-card suits then you open the higher-ranking.

4)	♠ A Q 7 6 2	5)	♠ J 7 6 5 4	6)	♠ A K Q 6 5
	♥ K Q 8 4 3		♥ A 2		♥ 7 2
	♦ 7 6		♦ A K 7 3 2		♦ 7
	♣ 3		♣ 7		♣ A K Q 6 5

With Hand **4)** open one heart. On Hands **5)** and **6)** open one spade.

Weak or strong no-trump?

The problem with opening the bidding comes when you do not have a five-card suit. When you have a balanced hand (ie one with no singleton and no more than one doubleton), then you either open the bidding with one no-trump, or else open a suit and then rebid one no-trump on the next round (or support partner). In the UK the majority of players open one no-trump with 12–14 points and rebid one no-trump with 15–17. However, generally speaking, worldwide and in particular in the USA most people prefer to open one no-trump with 15–17 points and rebid one no-trump with 12–14.

> **NOTE: In this book we are going to play a strong no-trump, opening one no-trump with 15–17 points.**

1)	♠ A 6 4	2)	♠ A K 6 2	3)	♠ 9 8 3
	♥ K Q 5 4		♥ 4 3		♥ K 5
	♦ K J 2		♦ A 10 7 3		♦ A Q 2
	♣ Q 10 3		♣ K Q 9		♣ A Q 8 4 3

All these hands are balanced with 15–17 points and should all be opened one no-trump.

Sometimes, however, you are dealt a hand that is a little off-centre, but is still in the 15–17 range and has no singleton.

4)	♠ A J 10 5 3	5)	♠ K 6	6)	♠ A Q
	♥ K 7 5		♥ A Q 7 6		♥ K 7 3
	♦ Q J 6		♦ K 10 8 5 4		♦ Q 6
	♣ A J		♣ K 10		♣ K J 8 7 4 2

These hands should also be opened one no-trump even though Hand **4)** has a five-card major, and Hands **5)** and **6)** have two doubletons. Remember that if you do not open one no-trump you cannot rebid one no-trump because that shows 12–14 points and these hands are too good. The subsequent auction is likely to be much easier if you open one no-trump in the first place.

Bridge is not a perfect science and the vocabulary is fairly limited. There are only 35 bids plus pass (and double and redouble), and many of those bids are rare. If you can get close to describing your hand with your opening bid then you should do so.

Limit bids vs forcing bids

After your opening bid, partner, if his hand is strong enough, will make a response. Before we go on to look at these responses to the various bids we must first discuss the concept of limit bids. A limit bid is one which describes accurately the strength of the hand in one go.

Some examples of limit bids are:

1)   An opening bid of one no-trump

2)   A response of one no-trump

3)   Any bid in partner's suit

An alternative to a limit bid is a forcing bid. A forcing bid is one which demands that partner should bid again. It may be stronger or weaker than a limit bid.

Some examples of forcing bids are:

1)   A new suit response to an opening bid in a suit

2)   A bid in a new suit by opener after a two-level change-of-suit response

If you have a choice between making a limit bid and a forcing bid, make the limit bid. If you can decribe your hand reasonably accurately in one bid then do so. The more bids you make in the auction the easier you make it for your opponents to defend.

Five-card majors

Most people who play a strong no-trump also like to play five-card majors. This means exactly what it sounds like: in order to open one heart or one spade you must hold at least five cards in the suit.

What if you don't have a five-card major

If you don't hold a five-card major and don't have the right strength for a one no-trump opening, you open your longer minor. With three cards in each minor, open one club. With four cards in each minor, open the stronger. Most of the time you will open a four-card or longer minor, but sometimes you will have to open a three-card suit.

This is not a disaster and it's worth it to know that your opening in a major shows five cards – particularly helpful if the opponents intervene. Minor suits are not as important as major suits. You need to bid and make eleven tricks for game in a minor suit, and even then you will not score as well as those who make game in a major or an overtrick in a no-trump game. Games in a minor suit are rare. If you open in a minor, partner will first investigate the possibility of a final contract in no-trumps or a major suit, so it is unlikely to matter that you have one card fewer than you might have in the minor you open.

1) ♠ K6   2) ♠ KQ76   3) ♠ KQ104
   ♥ A73   ♥ 763   ♥ AJ102
   ♦ AJ104   ♦ A85   ♦ K64
   ♣ Q932   ♣ A106   ♣ 87

With both four-card minors, Hand **1)**, open the stronger, one diamond. With both three-card minors, Hand **2)**, open one club. With three diamonds and only two clubs, Hand **3)**, open one diamond. This precise distribution is the only time you have to open one diamond on a three-card suit. Sometimes you are too strong to open one no-trump, not too weak. Open all the hands below one club:

4) ♠ KQJ5   5) ♠ 74   6) ♠ KQ42
   ♥ A43   ♥ AK87   ♥ AK106
   ♦ AK5   ♦ A86   ♦ 104
   ♣ Q103   ♣ AK32   ♣ AK4

Bidding after one no-trump

Balanced Hands

The opening one-trump bid is itself a limit bid. Most of the time partner will be able to place the final contract in one go. If partner has a balanced hand he should pass with fewer than 8 points since he knows that the most your side can have is 24. If he has 10 points he should raise to game in no-trumps because he knows you have at least 25. With 8 or 9 points he should raise to two no-trumps inviting you to bid game if you are maximum but pass if you are minimum. All raises of no-trump bids are limit bids.

On all these hands you should pass the one no-trump opening:

1)	♠ 762	**2)**	♠ 7632	**3)**	♠ QJ6
	♥ A32		♥ 652		♥ J4
	♦ Q54		♦ 982		♦ K543
	♣ 10762		♣ 763		♣ 9843

When you have at least 25 points between you and cannot have the 33 needed for a slam, raise straight to three no-trumps:

4)	♠ 854	**5)**	♠ A106	**6)**	♠ Q32
	♥ A7		♥ KJ5		♥ A7
	♦ J62		♦ Q84		♦ KJ104
	♣ KQ763		♣ J1043		♣ KQ76

When the strength of your hand is somewhere in the middle you should raise to two no-trumps, asking partner if he is minimum or maximum. However, I should stress that there is a bonus for bidding game, and two no-trumps is everyone's least favourite contract because it risks raising the level to one which may fail while not attracting a bonus. So don't push too hard to get to two no-trumps, and be prepared to gamble a little if you like your hand – after all, the opponents may not defend perfectly.

7)	♠ K 6	8)	♠ A 6 4	9)	♠ A 8
	♥ K 10 4		♥ J 8 7 2		♥ 10 6 5
	◆ K 7 4 3		◆ J 6 5		◆ 9 8 2
	♣ 9 8 6 4		♣ Q 5 2		♣ K Q 10 9 4

Hand **7)** is a dead centre raise of one no-trump to two no-trumps. On Hand **8)**, although you have 8 points I would pass one no-trump. You should devalue your hand for three reasons:

a) You have 4-3-3-3 distribution which is the worst there is.

b) You have no intermediate cards (tens and nines).

c) Your honour cards are in different suits and honour cards are generally more effective when they are working together.

With Hand **9)** go straight to three no-trumps yourself. Your good five-card club suit is well worth an extra point.

Let me explain further the point I made about Hand **8)**. If you have two (or three) four-card suits there will be a choice of suits for partner to develop in the play, and if you have a five-card suit it will generate, on average, one more trick than a four-card suit. Just one suit that is only four cards long, ie a 4-3-3-3 distribution, is the worst you can have.

If you are the one no-trump opener and your partner raises you to two no-trumps, generally speaking you should pass with 15 points and bid three no-trumps with 17. If you have 16 then you should value it in a similar way to that described opposite.

Unbalanced hands

As we have seen already, there are two things to discover in the bidding: first whether to play in a suit contract or no-trumps, and second at what level to play. For the vast majority of hands, all you need do is discover whether you have an eight-card major-suit. If you have you play in it; if you haven't you play in no-trumps. Only when you have extreme distribution or when you get into a competitive auction (see later) should you consider playing in a minor suit. If your hand is strong enough to invite game then you should be able to discover whether or not there is a fit before issuing your invitation, but on a weak hand you may have to guess.

When partner opens one no-trump and you have a five-card suit but insufficient points to be interested in game then you should bid your suit at the two level. This commands partner to pass. You do not know whether partner has two-, three- or four-card support for you. But even if he has only a doubleton your hand may well be more use in a suit contract than one no-trump. The odds favour you bidding your long suit. This bid is called a weakness take-out.

1)	♠ J 10 9 8 5	2)	♠ K 8 7 5 4	3)	♠ A K 8 7 3
	♥ 8 7 4		♥ J 6		♥ 6
	♦ 9 8 4 3		♦ 9 8 4		♦ 9 8 4 3
	♣ 4		♣ 10 6 5		♣ 10 6 5

Respond two spades on all these hands. On Hand **1)** you do not expect to make your contract but it will surely play better in spades than no-trumps. In no-trumps you have no entry and you will contribute nothing to partner's hand, but in spades you can well expect to contribute at least a couple of tricks. With a reasonably fitting hand opposite you may even make two spades. Hands **2)** and **3)** are somewhat stronger, but you still would not expect to make game, so sign off in two spades.

If you have a six-card major suit and enough points for game, then you can bid it directly. You know you have an eight-card fit because partner must have at least two cards in each suit to open one no-trump in the first place.

4)	♠ 5 4	5)	♠ 7 3	6)	♠ A 5 4
	♥ K J 9 7 5 4		♥ J 9 8 4 3 2		♥ K Q J 10 6 4
	♦ A 8 2		♦ A K 8 2		♦ K 5
	♣ Q 7		♣ 3		♣ 5

Bid four hearts on all these hands. Although Hand **5)** is a little short on values you have no way of knowing or discovering how well the hands fit. If your partner has lots of values in clubs with poor spades and hearts you may well go down, but if he has the right cards you could make a slam. Just go straight to game and hope for the best.

Note that this jump to game in your long suit applies only when your long suit is a major. It is different when your long suit is a minor.

7) ♠ 5 4	**8)** ♠ 7	**9)** ♠ 7 6
♥ Q 7	♥ K 7 6	♥ 9 8 2
♦ A 8 2	♦ K Q J 10 7 6 3	♦ A K Q 7 6 2
♣ K J 9 7 5 4	♣ 8 7	♣ 5 2

With these hands you should raise one no-trump directly to three. It may be wrong, but it's more likely that partner will make three no-trumps than that you'll make five of a minor. Even if three no-trumps is the wrong contract your opponents may not find the best lead.

We have now covered situations where you are weak and situations where you are strong with a six-card suit, but another common hand-type is when you have the values for game with a five-card major and don't know whether to bid game in your major or in no-trumps.

10) ♠ K J 7 6 3	**11)** ♠ Q J 5 4 2	**12)** ♠ K Q J 10 9
♥ Q 7 6	♥ K	♥ 8
♦ A 6	♦ A Q 7 6	♦ 9 5
♣ J 10 5	♣ 9 8 3	♣ A 8 7 4 3

In principle your bid with this type of hand is three of your major. This asks partner to raise you to game in the major with three- or four-card support, or to bid three no-trumps with only a doubleton. Bid three spades on Hands **10)** and **11)**. But you can always take a good idea too far and on Hand **12)** it would be silly to do anything but bid four spades. How is partner to know that a small doubleton is adequate support? Your spade suit is so strong and your hand so distributional that you are best to insist on game in spades.

Stayman

We have seen how to make sure we play in a 6-2 major-suit fit (by bidding game directly) and a 5-3 major-suit (by jumping in our long suit), but what about a 4-4 fit? Although it is not always so, generally the 4-4 major-suit fit will play better than no-trumps.

We locate a 4-4 major-suit fit by means of a conventional bid. A conventional bid is like a code: the meaning of the bid bears no relationship to what it actually says. When you have been playing bridge for a little longer you will discover many conventional bids, but this is perhaps the most common.

The conventional bid we use in this context is called the Stayman convention. Stayman is a bid of two clubs in response to one no-trump. It does not say that responder thinks he can make eight tricks with clubs as trumps, in fact it has nothing to do with clubs at all. It simply asks the opener if he holds a four-card major. The responses are simple: opener bids two hearts or two spades with four cards in that suit (two hearts with both), and two diamonds as a denial with no four-card major. After this, responder places the final contract in a similar way to that which we have seen.

1) ♠ K Q 7 6
    ♥ A K 3 2
    ♦ 9 8 3
    ♣ 10 6

2) ♠ A J 6 5
    ♥ 3 2
    ♦ K 7 6 3
    ♣ 9 8 2

3) ♠ Q 10 7 6
    ♥ 7
    ♦ A 5 3
    ♣ K Q 10 8 7

After partner opens one no-trump, you should bid two clubs on all these hands. On Hand 1) if partner responds two of either major you raise him to game in that suit. If he responds two diamonds, then you bid three no-trumps. On Hand 2) if he responds two spades then you raise him to game, but if he bids two hearts or two diamonds you simply rebid two no-trumps. If he is maximum he will raise you to three no-trumps, otherwise he will pass. If by any chance he has four spades as well as four hearts he will bid three or four spades, depending on whether he is minimum or maximum. After all, he knows that you have four spades, or you would not have bothered with Stayman. On Hand **3)** you raise a two-spade response to game, but bid three no-trumps over either two hearts or two diamonds. In this case, you will just have to keep your fingers crossed that partner has the heart suit adequately guarded.

Perhaps you are wondering what you bid in response to one no-trump if you want to make a weakness take-out into clubs. Well, in general you would only make a weakness take-out into a minor when you have a six-card suit, and what you must do is bid two clubs, Stayman, and then rebid three clubs over whatever partner says. It is not ideal to be a level higher than you would otherwise be, but the advantages of Stayman far outweigh the disadvantages.

4) ♠ 875	**5)** ♠ K873	**6)** ♠ J106
♥ 3	♥ Q10954	♥ K652
♦ 763	♦ 87	♦ J10987
♣ KJ10984	♣ 43	♣ 6

With Hand **4)** you bid two clubs in response to one no-trump and rebid three clubs whatever partner says. This tells him to pass. Although you would have preferred to play in two clubs, three clubs may make anyway, and if not, it might well be that you have kept your opponents out of a making contract.

With Hand **5)** you can also start with a Stayman two clubs. If partner bids two hearts or two spades you pass, while if he bids two diamonds you bid two hearts. This shows a five-card suit and he must pass.

With Hand **6)** you start with two clubs and pass whatever partner responds. You may end up in a seven-card fit in either spades or diamonds, but the odds are good that the final contract will be better than one no-trump.

Bidding after one of a suit

Raising partner

If you know you have an eight-card or longer major-suit fit and you can make a limit bid you should do so.

With three-card support		With four-card support	
6–9 points	raise to two	5–8 points	raise to two
10–12 points	raise to three	9–11 points	raise to three
13–15 points	raise to four	12–14 points	raise to four

Just as we have seen in hand evaluation in no-trump auctions, we can upgrade and downgrade hands from their basic point-counts.

Positive features are:
a) Shortages in side suits
b) Aces and kings rather than queens and jacks
c) Sources of tricks in side suits

Negative features are:
a) No ruffing value (ie 4-3-3-3 distribution – again)
b) Lots of queens and jacks, not with other honours
c) The honours spread about the hand rather than together

With the following hands raise a one spade opening to two spades:

1)	♠	Q76	**2)**	♠	J873	**3)**	♠	K76
	♥	A873		♥	A65		♥	6
	♦	K65		♦	10875		♦	A8732
	♣	652		♣	76		♣	7632

With the following three hands raise a one heart opening to three hearts:

4) ♠ K62
   ♥ A653
   ♦ K872
   ♣ 65 ♣

5) ♠ K106
   ♥ Q762
   ♦ 6
   KJ1076

6) ♠ K105
   ♥ QJ87
   ♦ QJ6
   ♣ QJ3

With the following hands raise a one spade opening to four spades:

7) ♠ AQ64
   ♥ K5
   ♦ K1032
   ♣ 872

8) ♠ KQ54
   ♥ AK76
   ♦ 54
   ♣ Q72

9) ♠ KJ1076
   ♥ A76
   ♦ 5
   ♣ J1065

Generally speaking, if you have four-card support and opening values, you should raise to four spades. You can add on a couple of points for five-card support, and a few more if you have a singleton, which makes **9)** a sound four spade bid.

If your partner has raised your one heart opening bid to two hearts, all that needs to be decided is whether or not you should bid on in the hope of reaching game. Remember that the minimum for partner's raise is 5 or 6 points, so to bid game with a balanced hand you need to be stronger that a one no-trump opening, ie about 18 points. If you are not balanced, it is a different matter altogether for the greater the fit you have the fewer high-card points you need for game.

Look at the following hands when partner raises one heart to two hearts:

10) ♠ K10
   ♥ KQ652
   ♦ AQ7
   ♣ AJ4

11) ♠ AQ54
   ♥ AK8743
   ♦ 6
   ♣ K6

12) ♠ 76
   ♥ AKJ87
   ♦ AQJ74
   ♣ 7

With Hand **10)** you have 19 points so should have enough for game, so bid four hearts. Hands **11)** and **12)** have fewer points, but both have huge potential and are worth four hearts. It is easy to think of minimum hands for partner which make game excellent.

If you have an ace or a king above what you would need for a minimum opening, say 15 or 16 points, you should ask partner's view on whether or not to press on to game. If you have a second suit you can bid it. This is forcing and asks partner to evaluate whether or not he fits with this suit. If you have no other suit then you can simply bid three of your suit and ask him whether he is minimum or maximum.

Here are some examples of in-between hands after your one spade opening has been raised to two spades:

13) ♠ A K 7 5 4 2	14) ♠ A Q J 7 6	15) ♠ K Q J 7 6
♥ A 6	♥ A 6 5 4	♥
♦ K J 3	♦ A 4	♦ Q 7 6 5 4
♣ 7 6	♣ 7 6	♣ K 5

With Hand **13)** bid three spades, asking partner to press on to game with a maximum, say 8 or 9 points. With Hand **14)** bid three hearts and with Hand **15)** bid three diamonds. These bids are called trial bids and ask partner to take a second look at his hand. He should bid game if he has two top honour cards that he knows are "working", ie aces, or the king of trumps, or the king of the second suit. If he has no known working cards he should sign off. If he has one working card, then he should look at his holding in the second suit – he should upgrade his hand if he has a queen in that suit, or if he has a doubleton.

Take a look at the following three hands and imagine that partner has opened one spade, you have raised to two spades and partner has continued with three diamonds:

16) ♠ K 7 6 2	17) ♠ J 7 6	18) ♠ A 8 4
♥ A 6 5 2	♥ K 5 4 2	♥ J 7 6 2
♦ 7 6 5	♦ Q 7	♦ Q 7
♣ 8 7	♣ J 7 6 2	♣ 9 8 4 3

With Hand **16)** you should accept any game try because you have two cards you more or less know will be helpful, and in addition you have a fourth trump and a possible ruffing value in clubs. You have the worst possible diamond holding but that does not matter when the rest of your hand is so suitable.

With Hand **17)** your hand is poor: only three trumps, no known useful ace or king. Although you have a useful diamond holding, sign off because the rest of your hand is so poor.

Hand **18)** is somewhere in the middle: only three trumps, but the ace of trumps is the most important card in the deck. You have an excellent diamond holding which will surely help partner establish his second suit so take the plunge and bid four spades.

When partner raises your one of a major opening to three, you just need something more than a rock-bottom minimum to accept. It is generally a good idea to bid on when you have a singleton more or less whatever your hand because it is a guess whether the hands will fit well and you may as well guess optimistically. So only pass with 12–14 points and no singleton, or a really horrible minimum with a singleton.

Responding in no-trumps

In order to respond to your partner's opening bid without a four-card fit you need 6 points. If you can bid a four-card suit at the one level you should do so, but you need 11 points to respond in a new suit at the two level (more about that later). So if you have 6–10 points and no suit that you can bid at the one level you respond one no-trump. The following are good examples of a one no-trump response to a one heart opening:

1) ♠ K J 4	**2)** ♠ Q 10 4	**3)** ♠ 6 5 4
♥ 6 3	♥ J 5	♥ 8
♦ Q 10 5 4	♦ A J 7 6	♦ A Q J 7 6
♣ J 10 5 4	♣ Q 7 6 2	♣ J 8 7 3

Hand **1)** is perfect: the prototype one no-trump bid. Hand **2)** is stronger but still not strong enough to respond at the two level. Hand **3)** is an example of how it is sometimes necessary to respond one no-trump with an unbalanced hand.

Responses of two no-trumps and three no-trumps are similar but they are stronger – 11–12 and 13–15 respectively – and should always be balanced. (Note that some textbooks recommend a 2NT response to be forcing.)

All no-trump responses are limit bids, and most of the time opener should be able to place the final contract. After a one no-trump response he would usually rebid a six-card suit, or bid a second four-card suit. With enough to invite game he can raise to two no-trumps or rebid three of his suit with a six-carder. A jump in a new suit is forcing to game, asking responder in the first instance to choose between the two suits.

After a two or three no-trump response, all bids in new suits below game level are forcing.

Responding in a new suit at the one level

In order to respond in a new suit at the one level you need at least 6 points and a four-card suit. But this new suit bid is forcing and not a limit bid, so there is no upper limit.

Generally speaking, unless you have the values for game, you should bid a major in preference to a longer minor. You should also bid a four-card major in preference to raising partner's minor – which may be only a three-card suit, remember. With 4-4 in the majors you respond one heart, but with 5-5 you respond one spade. That is because you intend to bid both suits when you are 5-5 and want to bid them in an economical order; when you are 4-4 you bid one heart to make it easy for partner to introduce spades when he does not have a balanced hand.

Here are some responding hands after partner has opened one diamond:

1)	♠ K J 87	2)	♠ A 632	3)	♠ A K 65
	♥ A 10 6 5		♥ 87		♥ A J 5
	♦ 76		♦ Q 7		♦ A 9 5 2
	♣ 983		♣ K J 10 5 4		♣ K 8

On Hand **1)** bid one heart, the lower major. Partner will rebid one spade if he has four of them.

On Hand **2)** bid one spade rather than two clubs. To bid clubs and then spades is forcing to game, so you would need a good 12 or more points for that. On Hand **3)** bid a quiet one spade for the time being. There is no need to panic just because you have a very strong hand. Partner is not allowed to pass your one spade response so you can bid more later.

Here are some more examples, this time after a one club opening:

4) ♠ J1054	**5)** ♠ KQ873	**6)** ♠ AQ76
♥ A84	♥ AQ762	♥ A75
♦ K10954	♦ 76	♦ KQJ107
♣ 7	♣ 8	♣ 7

With Hand **4)** you should bid one spade and pass if your partner rebids one no-trump. If you bid one diamond and he rebids one no-trump you may miss your spade fit.

With Hand **5)** respond one spade, intending to bid your hearts on the next round. Hand **6)** is the same shape as Hand **4)** but much stronger. Now you should start by bidding your diamonds because there might be a slam on.

> **NOTE: Always bid majors before minors unless you have the values to force to game.**

After a change of suit response at the one level, opener has several choices of rebid:

   a) He can rebid no-trumps
   b) He can rebid his own suit
   c) He can raise responder's suit
   d) He can bid a new suit

a) Rebidding no-trumps

A one no-trump rebid shows a weaker hand than opening one no-trump in the first place, ie 12–14 points.

Here are some example hands after the sequence: 1♣ – 1♦:

1) ♠ Q106   **2)** ♠ KJ95   **3)** ♠ A104
    ♥ K65   ♥ A732   ♥ 76
    ♦ J97   ♦ Q10   ♦ Q763
    ♣ AK73   ♣ K53   ♣ AK92

With Hand **1)** rebid one no-trump, showing a balanced hand in the 12–14 range. With Hand **2)**, should you bid one of your majors or one no-trump? We have seen earlier that partner will bid a major before diamonds unless he has the values for game. He cannot have a four-card major unless he intends to bid over one no-trump. So you should rebid one no trump. With Hand **3)** raise to two diamonds.

A jump two no-trump rebid shows a stronger hand than opening one no-trump in the first place, ie 18–19 points. Here are some examples after 1♣ – 1♥:

7) ♠ A104   **8)** ♠ AQ103   **9)** ♠ KJ104
    ♥ 76   ♥ K76   ♥ A
    ♦ KQ42   ♦ J106   ♦ AJ7
    ♣ AKQ5   ♣ AKQ   ♣ AQ104

I would rebid two no-trumps on all these, even with Hand **9)**. The chances of missing a 4-4 spade fit are now reduced because partner is likely to have enough to bid over two no-trumps. The advantage of two no-trumps is that it is a limit bid that describes the general nature of the hand accurately.

b) Rebidding the suit opened
A simple rebid of the suit opened usually shows a six-card suit and 11 to a poor 15 points. With a good 15 or more and a six-card suit, jump in the suit opened. Here are some examples after 1♣ – 1♠:

1) ♠ 87   **2)** ♠ A8   **3)** ♠ 8
    ♥ A87   ♥ A87   ♥ KJ76
    ♦ K3   ♦ K3   ♦ AQ7
    ♣ AQ10954   ♣ AQ10954   ♣ Q7643

Hand **1)** is a prototype two club rebid: 13 points and a good six-card suit. Add an ace, as in Hand **2)** and you have an excellent three club rebid. But Hand **3)** is a problem. If you rebid two clubs, partner is bound to be disappointed in the quality of your club suit as he will expect a hand more like **1)**. The alternative is to rebid one no-trump even with a singleton in partner's suit. In my opinion (though some would disagree), this is the better alternative – if you think your partner will not like it you can always missort your hand and apologise, saying that you had one of your clubs in with your spades!

c) Raising responder's suit

What you need to raise responder's suit is slightly different after a minor-suit opening than if you had opened one heart. If you opened one of a minor, you most often have a balanced hand and it is simply a question of whether you have a 4-4 major-suit or whether you play in no-trumps. So unless you have a distributional hand I would recommend that you need four-card support to raise.

When you have opened one heart it is slightly different; you are already known to hold five cards in hearts (compared with three for an opening in a minor). If you were to wait until you held four spades as well before raising partner, you would not raise him very often. With a balanced (5-3-3-2) hand and three-card support for partner I would raise whenever I held a small doubleton in one of the side suits. Some example hands:

1)	♠ A Q 7 5	**2)**	♠ J 7 6	**3)**	♠ K 7 6
	♥ 8 7 2		♥ A Q 2		♥ K J 8 7 2
	♦ K J 6		♦ Q 7		♦ A Q 2
	♣ K 6 5		♣ K J 8 7 2		♣ 8 7

On Hand **1)** you open one club and raise partner's one spade response to two spades, despite your 4-3-3-3 distribution. On Hand **2)** I would rebid one no-trump after opening one club. If partner is balanced with a poor four-card major I don't want him to struggle in two hearts or two spades when we could play happily in one no-trump. Some of the time that he has a five-card major he will bid again over one no-trump anyway. However, on Hand **3)**, having opened one heart, I would raise him to two spades. He should not expect more than three-card support for this sequence.

Just as you can make a jump rebid in no-trumps or your own suit, so can you make a jump raise in partner's suit. Add a little above a minimum opening to a little extra distribution and you have a single jump raise. With a full-blooded 18 count or so – or less with distributional compensation – you should raise him to game. Here are some example hands after the sequence 1♦ – 1♠:

4) ♠ A Q 7 6	**5)** ♠ A K 7 6	**6)** ♠ A K 8 7
♥ 6	♥ A Q 5	♥ A 6 5
♦ A K J 6 3	♦ K Q 5 4	♦ K Q 10 6 5
♣ 8 7 4	♣ 5 4	♣ 7

With Hand **4)** raise to three spades. You have only 14 points but it is so much better a hand than Hand **1)** above that you must make a jump raise. On Hand **5)**, with a full 18 points and a balanced hand you should raise to four spades. With partner having 6 or more you will have at least 24 between you which should be enough when you have a 4-4 fit. Hand **6)** is weaker in high-card points but much stronger in distribution, so is also worth a game raise.

d) Bidding a new suit

If you have an unbalanced hand with two (or even three) suits you can rebid in a new suit below the level of two of your first suit without showing any extra values. This bid in a new suit is not forcing, but partner should try to bid again if possible because you could have a very strong hand.

1) ♠ A Q 5 4	**2)** ♠ 7	**3)** ♠ K J 10 6
♥ 7	♥ A Q J 6 5	♥ 6
♦ J 10 3	♦ K J 6 5 2	♦ A Q 6 5
♣ K Q 6 5 4	♣ 8 7	♣ A 10 5 4

On Hand **1)** you open one club and rebid one spade when partner responds one heart. If partner had responded one spade you would have raised to two spades. On Hand **2)** you open one heart and rebid two diamonds when partner responds one spade. Hand **3)** is a three-suiter and they can be tricky. The usual recommendation is to open the suit below the singleton so you open one diamond and rebid one spade when partner responds one heart.

To make a bid in a suit that is higher than a simple rebid in the one you started with is a different matter. This shows extra values and is called a reverse. It is forcing for one round and shows about an ace more than a minimum opening, say 16 points or so.

Here are some more example hands:

4)	♠ A32	**5)**	♠ A5	**6)**	♠ 6
	♥ KQJ5		♥ 7		♥ KQJ5
	♦ 8		♦ KQ65		♦ AQ10763
	♣ AK652		♣ AK10762		♣ 76

With Hand **4)** you open one club. If partner responds one diamond, there is no problem and you rebid one heart. However, if he responds one spade you must rebid two hearts. The reason that this shows extra values is that if he prefers clubs (likely, since you have shown longer clubs than hearts) then he must go to the three level, in order to show you that preference. Hand **5)** is similar. You open one club and rebid two diamonds over either major-suit response from partner. On both Hands **4)** and **5)** you have shown your extra values. Partner must bid again, but it is now up to him to decide on the level and denomination. Hand **6)** is a different matter. You open one diamond and when partner responds one spade you must rebid two diamonds. You have nowhere near the 16 points needed for a reverse bid. If game is on for your side then partner will introduce hearts.

> **NOTE: Over a one-level response a reverse bid (bidding a suit at the two level above the level of the one opened) is forcing for one round, and promises at least five cards in the first suit.**

A jump bid in a new suit is forcing to game and hence shows about 19 or more points, or equivalent. Here are some examples:

7)	♠ A 4 2	8)	♠ -	9)	♠ 9
	♥ K Q J 10 8		♥ K Q J 10 7 6		♥ A Q
	♦ A K Q 8		♦ A K Q J 8		♦ A K Q 7 6
	♣ 7		♣ 8 7		♣ A J 9 8 2

On Hand **7)** open one heart and rebid three diamonds over a one spade response. If partner gives you preference to three hearts you can then show your spade support and leave the rest to partner. Hand **8)** has only 16 points but you more or less have game in your own hand. Rebid three diamonds over one spade, intending to bid four hearts on the next round. On Hand **9)** you should open one diamond and rebid three clubs over whichever major partner bids.

> **NOTE: A jump rebid by opener in a new suit is forcing to game.**

Responding in a new suit at the two level

All that we have learned so far about responding in a new suit at the one level and the continuing auction applies in a very similar fashion when the new suit response is at the two level, but there are differences.

a) A new suit at the two level shows 11 or more points

b) Unless the responding hand is extremely strong (16+) it also shows an unbalanced hand (otherwise the response would have been in no-trumps)

c) Because the initial response shows near opening values, all the rebids by opener which show extra values become forcing to game, for example, the sequence 1♥ – 2♣ – 3♥ is game-forcing (whereas 1♥ – 1♠ – 3♥ merely shows extra values), and 1♥ – 2♣ – 2♠ (a reverse after a two-level response) becomes game-forcing instead of merely forcing for one round.

Here are some examples of two-level responses after partner opens one heart:

1)	♠ A Q 7 6	2)	♠ 7 6	3)	♠ A 5 4
	♥ Q 4		♥ 8		♥ Q 7
	♦ A J 10 3 2		♦ A K J 8 5 2		♦ 6 5
	♣ 7 6		♣ Q 10 8 7		♣ A K J 10 6 5

With Hand **1)** you have enough to force to game so you should bid your longest suit first. Respond two diamonds. If partner rebids two hearts you can continue with two spades. If partner now bids two no-trumps you can raise to three no-trumps, while if he bids three diamonds you can press on with three hearts. You do not know what game is best so need to describe your hand to partner and let him decide.

Hand **2)** is a little light in terms of high cards for a two-level response but it is better than one no-trump with such a good suit and good distribution. You intend to rebid three diamonds whatever partner says. This shows invitational values and a good six-card suit and the rest is up to him. It is important that you do not rebid three clubs, because this would be forcing to game.

Hand **3)** is stronger. Bid two clubs intending to raise a two heart rebid to game, or two no-trumps to three no-trumps.

Other opening bids

There are two types of hand that we have yet to deal with:
    a) Hands that are too strong to be dealt with adequately by opening at the one level
    b) Hands that are not strong in terms of high-card points but have good distribution; judicious bidding on this type of hand can make life very difficult for the opponents.

The two no-trump opening

This is very like the one no-trump opening but a level higher. It shows 20–22 points and a balanced hand. Here are some examples of two no-trump openers:

1) ♠ A Q J 5　　**2)** ♠ A J 10 6 5　　**3)** ♠ 8 7
　　♥ K 10 4　　　　　♥ K 7　　　　　　♥ A K Q J
　　♦ A J 10 5　　　　♦ A Q 5　　　　　♦ K Q J 7
　　♣ A Q　　　　　　♣ A Q 7　　　　　♣ A J 9

The bidding over two no-trumps is very similar to over one no-trump except that there is no weakness take-out. This is because it is more important to be able to offer partner a choice of game than to be able to settle in a partscore after such a strong opening. All responses are forcing to game.

Here are some examples of responding hands:

4) ♠ J 7 6　　**5)** ♠ Q J 8 7　　**6)** ♠ Q J 10 6 5
　　♥ 9 8　　　　　♥ K 10 7 6　　　　♥ A 6 2
　　♦ 10 7 6 4 3　　♦ 9 8 7　　　　　♦ 8 7 3 2
　　♣ J 6 2　　　　♣ 8 2　　　　　　♣ 7

On Hand **4)** pass and hope for the best. Even if you could bid a weak three diamonds there's no certainty that it would be a better contract than two no-trumps. On Hand **5)** bid three clubs, Stayman, just as over one no-trump but a level higher. If partner shows a major, raise him to game, or bid three no-trumps. On Hand **6)** bid three spades. Partner will choose between four spades and three no-trumps.

The two club opening

Sometimes you are too strong even for a two no-trump opening, or maybe you have a huge distributional hand. This is the time to bring in the big guns. An opening bid of two clubs is a special conventional bid that shows an extremely strong hand. It is totally artificial and says nothing whatsoever about clubs. Unless the rebid is two no-trumps (showing 23–24 points) when responder may pass, it is unconditionally forcing to game. However weak responder is he must keep on bidding until game is reached.

Here are some examples of two club openings:

1) ♠ A K 6	**2)** ♠ A K Q J 6	**3)** ♠ A K Q J
♥ K Q J 9 4	♥ A Q J 5	♥ K Q J 10 6 3
♦ K Q 5	♦ A K 4	♦ A K 2
♣ A J	♣ 7	♣ –

On Hand **1)** open two clubs intending to rebid two no-trumps. That is the only rebid partner is allowed to pass. If you had a couple of points more you would have to rebid three no-trumps.

Hands **2)** and **3)** are much stronger. In both instances start by rebidding your longest suit. Partner must keep the bidding open until you reach game.

The most frequent response to two clubs is two diamonds. In the early days of bridge this was used to show a negative, ie fewer than some number of points. However, these days it is generally considered a bad idea to respond other than two diamonds unless you have a good suit of your own. By bidding anything else you make it harder for partner to show his hand. So you should always bid two diamonds unless you have a suit headed by two of the top three honours when it would be fine to bid a five-card suit at the two level or a six-card suit at the three level.

Here are some examples of responding hands:

4) ♠ 4 3 2	**5)** ♠ K 7 6 3	**6)** ♠ K Q J 6 5
♥ 4 3 2	♥ Q 6 5	♥ 7 6 2
♦ 4 3 2	♦ K 6 5	♦ 8 2
♣ 5 4 3 2	♣ Q 9 2	♣ 8 3 2

With Hand **4)** you must resist all temptation to pass. The two club opening is forcing. You must bid two diamonds. You must not pass on the next round either – at least not unless partner rebids two no-trumps. However much you hate your hand you must keep on bidding until game is reached.

It is unusual to hold as many high-card points facing a two club opener as there are in Hand **5)**, but even if you do you should still respond two diamonds. You must find out why partner opened two clubs and something about his distribution before you can hope to work out the best final contract.

Although Hand **6)** has fewer high-card points, they are all concentrated in one suit and it would be helpful to tell partner this, so respond two spades to let him know about your good suit.

Opening two diamonds/ hearts/ spades

These opening bids do not show good hands at all; they show hands of around 6–10 high-card points with a good six-card suit. When you make one of these openings it will sometimes make it easier for your side to bid to its best contract, but more often it will make life difficult for the opponents. Instead of having lots of space to conduct an accurate auction, perhaps starting with a one club opening, they suddenly find that you have bid, say, two spades, and they have to start their auction at the three level (or with two no-trumps). Here are some examples of weak two openings:

1) ♠ K Q 10 9 5 2   **2)** ♠ J 10 5   **2)** ♠ 8 7
   ♥ J 4 3   ♥ A K J 10 5 4   ♥ K 7 6
   ♦ 5   ♦ 6 2   ♦ A J 10 8 7 3
   ♣ 8 4 2   ♣ 8 7   ♣ 10 2

Hand **1)** is an example of a minimum weak two spade bid. Hand **2)** is a maximum two heart bid, and Hand **3)** is a goodish two diamond opening.

In response to these weak two openings, partner will often be able to bid the final contract immediately. If he has a strong hand he can introduce a new suit of his own which is forcing, just as over a one-level opening. However, if he wants to find out just how good a weak two bid you hold because he has some sort of fit and is interested in a game or a slam, he can bid two no-trumps as an enquiry. In response to this two no-trump bid, opener rebids his suit with a minimum and bids a high-card feature with an above minimum. With an excellent suit headed by two of the top three honours he raises to three no-trumps and lets responder choose the final contract.

On the hands above he would rebid three spades on Hand **1)**, three no-trumps with Hand **2)** and three hearts with Hand **3)**.

These opening bids of two diamonds, two hearts and two spades are limit bids. Once you have opened with one of these bids, unless partner asks you a direct question (via the two no-trump enquiry) or bids a new suit which is forcing, you should not bid again. If partner makes a penalty double you should trust him to know what he is doing. Too often people use these openings to get the opponents into trouble but then undo all the good work by bidding again.

> **NOTE: Once you have opened a weak two bid leave the rest to partner unless he invites your opinion.**

Higher opening bids

These are very similar to weak two bids but tend to have more distribution and longer suits. The exact strength depends to some extent on the vulnerability. If all goes wrong and partner has an unsuitable hand for you and you are doubled, you don't want to lose too much compared with the opponents' game contract. If the opponents are vulnerable you should be prepared to risk losing 800 (it's worth risking a small loss in the hope that they will go wrong), but if they are non-vulnerable you should not lose more than 500. Again, it is important that once you have launched your missile (the three or four level opening), you then keep quiet. If partner bids three no-trumps you pass; if partner doubles the opponents you pass; if

partner raises you to game and the opponents bid you pass.
Here are some examples of high-level openings:

1) ♠ K Q J 9 8 3 2   2) ♠ 8 7 2   3) ♠ –
   ♥ 7 6 2   ♥ A K Q J 7 6 2   ♥ 8 3
   ♦ 4   ♦ 7   ♦ K Q J 8 7 6 2
   ♣ 8 3   ♣ 6 5   ♣ J 7 6 2

Hand **1)** has six tricks: OK for a four spade opening non-vulnerable
against vulnerable, or three spades at equal vulnerability. Hand **2)** has
seven tricks, enough for four hearts at all but vulnerable against not.
Hand **3)** is a bit of an oddity; I'd open five diamonds at favourable
vulnerability and four diamonds at equal.

Strong hands

The most exciting times at bridge are when you and your partner have
strong hands that fit together well and you can make a slam. We have
seen how to deal with some strong opening hands already, but
sometimes it is responder who has more than his share of goodies.

Jump-shift responses

When your partner opens the bidding and you have such a good hand
that you immediately start thinking about a slam, it can be a good
idea to tell partner this by jumping the bidding in a new suit
immediately. This is called a jump-shift. In the old days it was
considered normal to make a jump-shift response whenever you had
a strong hand, but these days the fashion is only to make such a
response if you know where you are going, so you should have one of
the following three hand-types:
  a) A fit for partner (support partner on the next round).
  b) An excellent suit of your own that needs no support from partner
  (bid your suit again on the next round).

c) A good five- or six-card suit in a balanced hand (bid no-trumps next time).

With other strong hands, start with a simple response and make your slam move later when you know more about partner's hand. The following hands are all suitable for a jump-shift response of two spades if partner opens one heart:

1) ♠ A K 7 6 4 **2)** ♠ A K Q J 10 7 2 **3)** ♠ K Q J 10 6
  ♥ K Q 5 4   ♥ 4   ♥ Q 6
  ♦ K 5 4   ♦ A 5 4   ♦ A Q 5
  ♣ 6   ♣ Q 5   ♣ A 10 5

With Hand **1)** you will next support his hearts. With Hand **2)** you intend to rebid your spades. With Hand **3)** you intend to rebid no-trumps. Suppose now that you have decided on trumps, and know that you are in the slam zone; there are two possible ways to proceed.

Blackwood

Along with Stayman, Blackwood is perhaps one of the most popular conventions worldwide. There are countless variations on the basic theme but here we will deal with the straightforward kind. When you have agreed trumps and know you are in the slam zone but just want to make sure that there are not two aces missing, you can use a bid of four no-trumps to find out. This four no-trump bid asks for aces and partner responds in the following way:

5♣ shows zero or four aces (in practice it is always easy to work out which)

5♦ shows one ace

5♥ shows two aces

5♠ shows three aces

If you discover that all the aces are held you can proceed with five no-trumps. This asks partner to bid the grand slam if he can (maybe all he needs to know is that there are no aces missing), otherwise he shows how many kings he has in a similar manner:

6♣ shows no kings
6♦ shows one king
6♥ shows two kings
6♠ shows three kings

Here are a couple of example hands.

1)
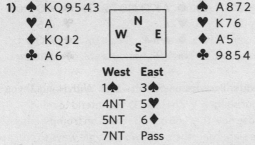

West	East
1♠	3♠
4NT	5♥
5NT	6♦
7NT	Pass

Once East shows primary spade support and good values, West is prepared to ask for aces. To his pleasant surprise East admits to holding two. West could now bid the small slam with confidence, but it is just possible that East holds a king to go with his two aces, so West bids five no-trumps to ask for kings. When East admits to a king, West can count thirteen tricks and bids the grand slam.

2)
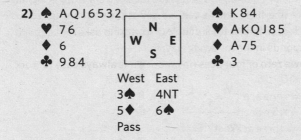

West	East
3♠	4NT
5♦	6♠
Pass	

The trump suit does not have to be explicitly agreed. Any jump to four no-trumps after partner has just bid a suit should be taken as Blackwood. Here, West's three spade opener shows a weak hand with a good seven-card suit. Provided West's spades are headed by the ace, East can count plenty of tricks, so he tries four no-trumps. When West shows an ace – almost certainly the ace of spades – East knows there is a small slam, but knows that the opponents hold an ace. So he bids six spades.

Blackwood is one of the most misused conventions in the world. It should be used only when the trump suit is known and when the answer to the question is helpful. It is wrong to use Blackwood when:

a) You have a void.

b) You have no control (ace, king or singleton) in an unbid suit, ie you need to know where partner's honours are, not just how many he holds.

c) You need partner's co-operation to help you decide whether a slam is on.

Cue-bids

Cue-bids are what you need when Blackwood is no use. Blackwood needs one player to take control and ask the relevant question, while cue-bidding is a conversation between the two players. When one suit is agreed as trumps, there is no point in looking for another fit, so a bid in a new suit at the four level or higher shows a control (ace, king, singleton or void) and suggests the idea of a slam. If partner also likes the idea of a slam then he can cue-bid in like manner, or even use Blackwood himself. Here are a couple of examples:

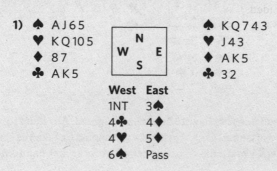

1)

	West		East
♠	A J 6 5	♠	K Q 7 4 3
♥	K Q 10 5	♥	J 4 3
♦	8 7	♦	A K 5
♣	A K 5	♣	3 2

West	East
1NT	3♠
4♣	4♦
4♥	5♦
6♠	Pass

When West hears his partner bid three spades over the one no-trump opening, asking him to choose between three no-trumps and four spades, he has such a good hand that he can envisage a slam if his partner has extra values. So he bids four clubs. This shows spade support (otherwise he would simply rebid three no-trumps) and also a maximum one no-trump opener that includes the ace of clubs.

East is not ashamed of his hand and co-operates with a return cue-bid of four diamonds. West is still there and owns up to his king of hearts. East is optimistic but not quite confident enough to bid the slam so he bids five diamonds, saying that he has the king of diamonds as well as the ace. That is enough for West who now bids the slam.

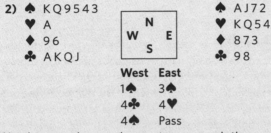

2)
	West		East
♠	KQ9543	♠	AJ72
♥	A	♥	KQ54
♦	96	♦	873
♣	AKQJ	♣	98

West	East
1♠	3♠
4♣	4♥
4♠	Pass

West has great hopes when partner responds three spades, but needs to find out if East has a control in diamonds, so he cue-bids four clubs. But when East can only bid four hearts (he would bid four diamonds with both red kings), West signs off in four spades and the bad slam is avoided.

Chapter 6

The competitive auction

All the bidding that we have seen so far has been in an uncontested auction. You open the bidding, partner responds etc, and eventually, after exchanging as much information as you can manage, you get to choose your final contract. Unfortunately, in the real world, the other side are allowed to bid too. At least half the hands become a bit of a free-for-all, with both sides jostling each other, trying to get the biggest plus score for their side. Bid too much and you may get doubled and lose a penalty; don't bid enough and you let the opponents play at too comfortable a level and maybe don't even bid and make your own contract.

Priorities change in the contested auction. It is important to describe your hand to partner as quickly as possible so he can decide whether to defend or bid on. There is no time for delicate auctions, you have to bid what you hope you can make. Don't let the opponents make you guess – you want it to be them who have to do the guessing.

Here are some guidelines for successful competitive bidding:

a) Support partner's suit if you possibly can.

b) Bid a lot if you have a good fit for partner, but be restrained without a fit.

c) Be more swayed by your distribution than your high-card points.

d) Once you have made your opponents guess, shut up; if you bid again you may let them recover even if they guessed wrong before.
    NOTE: When the opponents have entered the auction try to bid your hand to the limit immediately if you possibly can.

Overcalls

An overcall is a bid that is made after an opponent has opened the bidding. An overcall should be made for one of three reasons:
    a) In the hope of buying the contract.
    b) In the hope of making life difficult for your opponents.
    c) In order to help partner with his eventual opening lead.
An overcall can be made on less than an opening bid, but not a lot less unless it is a good suit that you want partner to lead.

A jump overcall is a weak, distributional, disruptive tool, just like the opening bids of two, three and four. So if you have a six-card or longer suit and fewer than opening values in high cards your intention should be to disrupt the opponents' auction, and you should make some sort of jump overcall. But, as with the weak opening bids, you have to pay some attention to the vulnerability. If you are too afraid to make a jump overcall you are better to pass and not give away information about the distribution to the eventual declarer.

If you are going to stretch to make a one-level overcall, then make sure it takes away some bidding space. For example, it is more disruptive to overcall an opening bid of one club with one spade than with one diamond. Your one diamond overcall should show a good hand or a good suit.

A two-level simple (ie not a jump) overcall is a fairly serious proposition. Partner will expect a six-card suit for a two-level bid, and will note that you did not jump so you should have a good hand. If the overcall is in a minor and he has some sort of fit he will start thinking about three no-trumps, and your hand should not be too much of a disappointment to him.

Let's look at some examples:

1) ♠ A K 10 6 5   2) ♠ 8 7 2   3) ♠ 7
   ♥ 8 7 2   ♥ 6 3   ♥ K Q J 10 7 6
   ♦ 6 3   ♦ A K 10 6 5   ♦ 8 7 3
   ♣ 8 7 2   ♣ 8 7 2   ♣ 6 3 2

With Hand **1)** you should bid one spade over any opening bid non-vulnerable. The power of the spade suit is huge because it outbids every other suit at the same level. Vulnerable it is more dangerous because partner might bid too much and you could get doubled and lose a big penalty. It is safer to pass. On Hand **2)** I would not overcall one diamond over one club at any vulnerability. It takes no space away, it gives away information and my partners are good enough at opening leads not to need too much help. As for overcalling at the two level over a major-suit opening, don't even think about it.

With Hand **3)** it is a jump overcall or none at all. A two-level non-vulnerable jump overcall is perfect but otherwise it's a bit pushy. Just don't overcall at the one level – partner will never guess your hand.

4) ♠ A K J 4 3   5) ♠ 6 5   6) ♠ A K 6
   ♥ Q 10 6 5   ♥ A Q 7 6 2   ♥ 6 5
   ♦ 6 5 2   ♦ K J 10 6   ♦ K 8 7 3 2
   ♣ 7   ♣ 9 2   ♣ A 3 2

Hand **4)** is a fine one spade overcall over any opening bid at any vulnerability. Hand **5)** is a good one heart overcall but a dreadful two heart overcall. At the two level you need a six-card suit. Hand **6)** is similar; if the opponents open one club it is fine to overcall one diamond, but if they open in a major you should pass.

7) ♠ 6 5   8) ♠ Q 7 6 2   9) ♠ A Q 3
   ♥ K 6   ♥ A K 6   ♥ K J 10 6
   ♦ A K 10 6 5 2   ♦ A 10 5   ♦ K 10 2
   ♣ 7 5 3   ♣ J 10 3   ♣ K J 4

Hand **7)** is a normal two diamond overcall over a major-suit opening, though it is a little frisky vulnerable. On Hand **8)**, even though you have opening values you have to pass as you have no suit to bid. However, when the hand gets stronger as **9)** here, and you have a stopper in the suit opened, you can overcall one no-trump, which shows just a tiny bit more than a one no-trump opener (a good 15 to 18 points). After you overcall one no-trump the bidding continues just as if you had opened one no-trump, with two clubs Stayman.

Responding to overcalls

Raising the overcall: Once the opponents have opened the bidding it is not likely that your side has a game on unless you have a fit, so the most likely response to the overcall is a raise. You should raise to the same level as you would have done had the overcall been an opening bid.

Responding in no-trumps: There should be no need to "rescue" partner from his overcall as he should have a good suit; and there is no need to keep the bidding open because the upper limit for an overcall is less than the upper limit of an opening bid. A one no-trump response shows a little more than after an opening bid, say 9–11 points, and a 2NT response 12–13.

Bidding a new suit: Occasionally you will have a good suit of your own that you want to introduce. A change of suit after an overcall shows a good suit and a good hand but is not absolutely forcing. If your partner makes such a change of suit you should find another bid if you possibly can but if not a pass is acceptable with a minimum overcall.

The take-out double

Sometimes you have a hand that looks suitable for bidding on after the opponents have opened but you don't have a suit to bid. There is a convention to help with this type of problem, and it is called the take-out double. The technical meaning of a double is to double the stakes, ie it would be made on a hand where you did not think that the opponents would make their contract. However, it is very unlikely that you would have a hand that could be that confident about defeating a one-level suit contract. So, a long time ago someone came up with the bright idea that a double of a suit opening should not be for penalties but for take-out.

This double shows about opening values or more and asks partner to bid his best suit.

Here are some example hands after a one heart opening:

1) ♠ A J 6 5   2) ♠ A 10 5 4   3) ♠ K J 5
    ♥ 6   ♥ 9 3   ♥ 6
    ♦ K J 10 5   ♦ K Q 4   ♦ A K 7 6 2
    ♣ A 8 7 2   ♣ A K 6 5   ♣ K 10 6 5

Hand **1)** is perfect for a take-out double of one heart, but Hands **2)** and **3)** are fine too. It is preferable to have four cards in the unbid major but good three-card support is acceptable when the hand is otherwise suitable.

4) ♠ J 7 6 5   5) ♠ A Q 7 6 3   6) ♠ K J 10 3
    ♥ A Q 4   ♥ 6   ♥ 5 4
    ♦ Q J 5   ♦ K Q 3   ♦ K 4
    ♣ K 7 3   ♣ Q J 3 2   ♣ A Q 7 3 2

Hand **4)** is too balanced for a take-out double of one heart – or anything else for that matter! If the opponents bid to a high level in hearts partner is too likely to join in in spades, not expecting you to hold so much defence against hearts.

With Hand **5)** you should simply overcall one spade. A take-out double should deny five cards in a major that could be overcalled at the one level (unless it is a very strong hand).

You would like to join in the auction with Hand **6)** but the trouble with making a take-out double is that partner might respond in diamonds and end up playing in a 4-2 fit. However, bridge is not an exact science and the hand is not very suitable for a one spade overcall (only a four-card suit) or two clubs (not a good enough suit) either. And if you pass you could easily miss a contract your way. Often you have to make the best of an unpalatable selection and here I would risk a double, hoping that partner would not bid diamonds unless he had five.

> **NOTE: A double of a suit opening is for take-out but a double of a one no-trump opening is a penalty double.**

Responding to a take-out double

The first thing to say about responding to a take-out double is that you must. Partner is asking you to bid and unless you have a tremendously strong holding in the opponent's suit, that is what you must do.

Here are some hands you might hold when partner makes a take-out double of a one spade opening:

1)	2)	3)
♠ 5 4 3 2	♠ J 5 2	♠ Q J 10 9 8 7
♥ 4 3 2	♥ 6 5 2	♥ 7 6
♦ 4 3 2	♦ K 10 5 4	♦ Q 8 2
♣ 4 3 2	♣ J 10 4	♣ 3 2

Hand **1)** is everyone's nightmare. Not only do you have a complete Yarborough, you don't even have a four-card suit to bid. But you must not pass. Bid your lowest three-card suit, two clubs.

Hand **2)** is fine. You have a smattering of points and a fairly decent four-card suit. Bid two diamonds quite happily.

Hand **3)** is what you need to pass: really good spades. Partner should lead a spade if he has one and you should try to draw declarer's trumps as quickly as you can. Then your partner will be able to make all his lovely winners in the outside suits.

Because you don't need any values at all to respond to a take-out double, when you do have a decent hand you have to make some show of strength. You need about 8 points and a five-card suit to jump the bidding, or 10 points and a four-card suit. If you have 8–10 points and good stoppers in the opponent's suit you can respond one-trump, and with more you can jump.

Here are some stronger responding hands after partner has made a take-out double of one heart:

4)	♠ A Q 4 3	5)	♠ 6 5	6)	♠ A 4
	♥ 7 6 3 2		♥ K Q 10 7		♥ 9 8 4 3
	♦ K 10 3		♦ Q J 10 3		♦ K Q 10 7 6
	♣ 6 5		♣ J 5 4		♣ 7 6

With Hand **4)** you are just about worth two spades. I know I said 10 points with a four-card suit but it is always better to bid the other major than a minor. This is partly because partner is more likely to hold the other major, and partly because game in a major requires you to make only ten tricks, rather than eleven in a minor.

Hand **5)** is perfect for one no-trump: 9 points and plenty of stoppers in the suit partner will be short in.

Hand **6)** is a good example of a three diamond bid. If partner has extra values and a heart stopper and bids three no-trumps the diamond suit will come in handy for tricks; on the other hand, if partner has a singleton heart and wants to look for a game in diamonds, your hand is suitable for that too.

Take-out doubles with strong hands

Every now and then after an opponent opens with one of a suit you find you are looking at a very strong hand. The upper limit for a simple overcall is about 17 points, so what do you do if you have more than that? The answer is that you can start with a take-out double, even if you do not have the right distribution. If you are strong and your right-hand opponent has opening values, the chances are high that partner will make a simple response in a suit and then you can bid your own suit. This sequence of actions shows a hand too strong to overcall in the first place.

Here are some example hands:

1)	♠ A K Q J 5	2)	♠ A Q 4	3)	♠ 7
	♥ A 6 5		♥ K Q 10		♥ K Q J 8 7 6
	♦ 6		♦ K Q 10 6 5		♦ A K 5
	♣ A J 10 5		♣ A 5		♣ A Q 2

Hand **1)** is too strong for a one spade overcall over any opening bid, so start with a double, intending to rebid spades whatever partner's response.

Hand **2)** is suitable for no-trumps but a one no-trump overcall shows only 15–18 points, so double first and then bid no-trumps to show a stronger hand. Hand **3)** is too strong for two hearts over one spade, so double first and bid hearts later.

When opponents intervene

So how does the opponents' interruption of your auction affect your bidding? Well, in general terms, it becomes more important to describe your hand as accurately as possible in one go. When one opponent intervenes there is a greater likelihood that the other one will raise the ante by joining in too and if you don't take the chance to describe your hand quickly it may be much more difficult on the next round.

As in competitive bidding in general, distribution and fit count for more than high-card points. If you had been going to raise your partner's one spade opening to two spades but your opponent comes in with three diamonds, then generally you take a deep breath and bid three spades – but not if your hand looks good for defending against diamonds.

The bigger the fit you have the bigger the fit they have (and vice versa). If both sides have a good fit it becomes more likely that both sides can make contracts – partscores, games or even, in extreme situations, slams. If both sides can make contracts then it is important to buy the hand. However, in a competitive bidding battle, if the hands are more balanced it does not usually matter too much who wins because if, say, three hearts is making, then three spades will go down, or vice versa.

Here are some hands you might hold when your partner opens one heart and the next hand overcalls two clubs:

1)	♠ Q10652	2)	♠ J763	3)	♠ 873
	♥ A76		♥ A6		♥ J105
	♦ 76		♦ QJ4		♦ 754
	♣ J104		♣ AQ93		♣ KQ73

With Hand **1)** you would have bid one spade without the overcall, but now it is important to support partner's known five-card suit. If they bid on to three diamonds partner needs to know you have support or he will not be able to push on to three hearts when it is right for him to do so.

With Hand **2)** you would have bid one spade without the intervention but now a simple three no-trumps is a much better idea. Tell partner in one go that you have a balanced 13–15 points with at least two club stoppers. If you bid spades partner might raise you with three-card support and a singleton club.

With Hand **3)** you would have raised hearts before the overcall but now it is wiser to pass. Partner won't expect you to have all those values in clubs. If you raise and the next hand bids three clubs, partner, who is likely to be void, will probably bid too high in hearts.

The negative (or Sputnik) double

Just as some bright spark decided many years ago that it was more useful for a double to be for take-out than for penalties after an opening bid in a suit, so a different genius came up with the same idea after intervention.

I have written of the need to make a descriptive bid in one go after intervention but what do you do when your hand is not describable in one bid? New suits tend to show five-card suits in competitive auctions, so what do you bid when you don't have a five-card suit or a stopper in the suit overcalled? Similarly, if an opponent intervenes so that you have to bid your suit at the two level when you were only worth a one-level response, what do you do? If you pass, partner will not know that you have anything at all, and if you bid – which is forcing for one round, as without the intervention – partner may rebid two no-trumps with a balanced 12-count and you will be too high.

The answer is to use a take-out double to help you with these problem hands. If you have a five-card suit and the values to bid at whatever level you are at, then that is what you do, otherwise you double. In response to this double, partner makes his natural rebid and you proceed from there – but all the time partner knows that your hand does not fulfil the requirements for some other natural action.

Here are some examples of negative doubles after partner has opened one club and your right-hand opponent has overcalled one spade:

1) ♠ 76
   ♥ AQ76
   ♦ K54
   ♣ J1076

2) ♠ 76
   ♥ KQJ107
   ♦ Q532
   ♣ 65

3) ♠ A4
   ♥ KQ73
   ♦ A65
   ♣ Q1065

It is usual for a take-out double of a simple overcall to promise four cards (or more) in any unbid major(s). Hand 1) is a textbook example. You would be happy to hear partner rebid one no-trump, two clubs or two hearts. And if he has extra values and wants to invite game you would be pleased to accept.

On Hand 2) you would like to bid your hearts but you are not strong enough to bid at the two level. Double first and then bid two hearts. Partner will know you have a good suit but are not very strong.

Negative doubles can be made on very strong hands. Double with Hand **3)** and plan to show your strength later by raising anything partner says to game.

Now let's look at it from the other side of the table. Suppose you open one club and your left-hand opponent overcalls one spade. Partner doubles and the next hand passes. What do you bid with?

4)	♠ A Q 5	**5)**	♠ A 5	**6)**	♠ A 5
	♥ 4 3 2		♥ K J 10 4		♥ K 7 6 3
	♦ J 10 5		♦ Q 5 4		♦ 7 6
	♣ A Q 10 5		♣ Q 10 4 2		♣ A K J 8 2

With Hand **4)** you simply rebid one no-trump. You have a double stopper in spades and 12–14 points, what could be better?

Hand **5)** is similar but your stopper is weaker and you have four hearts. Since partner has promised four hearts too you know there is a 4-4 fit and should bid two hearts. That contract is likely to play several tricks better than one no-trump.

Hand **6)** is too good to bid two hearts; it is not only a full king stronger than **5)**, but it also has good distribution. Bid three hearts, just as you would have done if there had been no intervention and partner had responded one heart.

Now, if you are going to double the overcall with hands like we have seen on the previous page, you cannot also double when you have good values and a strong holding in the opponent's suit.
So, what would you bid after 1♣ – 1♠ with?

7)	♠ K J 10 6 5 2	**8)**	♠ A Q J 9 4	**9)**	♠ A 10 4 3 2
	♥ 5 4		♥ 5 4		♥ K 5
	♦ 4 3 2		♦ 9 8 4		♦ Q 2
	♣ 6 5		♣ A 6 3		♣ K J 10 7

With Hand **7)** you pass. If partner is short in the opponent's suit, then he should bid again, usually with a double. Then you pass and hope to collect a decent penalty despite your lack of high cards.

Similarly with Hand **8)** you pass. Partner must not pass out one spade with two cards or fewer in the suit overcalled. When he doubles you pass and defend one spade doubled.

Hand **9)** is a close decision. It certainly could be right to defend one spade doubled, but my preference would be for a direct three no-trumps instead. The spade spot cards are not strong, and if partner really has a club suit then we might have too good a fit to make defending one spade very profitable. Don't get greedy – go for the more or less sure game instead

Perhaps we should now take a look at opener's action on the second round. It may go against the grain to bid again with minimum values, but if you are short in the suit overcalled, you must do just that. Here are some example hands after the auction 1♣ – 1♠ – Pass – Pass:

10) ♠	6 4	**11)** ♠	-	**12)** ♠	Q 8 6
♥	K J 6 5	♥	K J 10 3	♥	5
♦	A Q 5	♦	K 6 5	♦	A Q 5 4
♣	K 8 7 2	♣	A Q J 7 6 3	♣	A J 8 7 4

With Hand **10)** you should double. If the opponents have stopped in one spade partner must have fair values and the reason for his pass must be because he has length in spades. You have nothing to be afraid of if partner wishes to defend one spade doubled, so double for him.

With Hand **11)** you also suspect that partner has passed because he is hoping to take a penalty from one spade. However, you fear he might be disappointed with the outcome. He does not yet know that you have such an unbalanced hand, so now is the time to enlighten him. Rebid two hearts. He will know that you also have long clubs and he should be able to choose the final contract.

With Hand **12)** you should pass happily. It is unlikely that partner has five spades when you have three (and if he has you know the opponents are not in their best contract so defending undoubled should be profitable). It is more likely that partner has a poor hand and the opponents may have missed game.

Chapter 7

The way forward

So you've read and understood the book. You now know how to play bridge. Where do you go from here?

To start with, there is a great deal of learning still to do. bridge is a complex game. Even the best players in the world would acknowledge that they still have a lot to learn. And the game changes. When I began to play, the goal was steady, error-free bridge. Now it is very different. The opposition enter your auctions with gay abandon, forcing the bidding level up and making you guess when before you could have explored at leisure. Now the bidding is about making life difficult for opponents and learning how to give information only when it will be of more use to partner than to the opponents.

The way to improve and understand the game more is to play. The more you play the better you will become. If you really want to improve, find a partner with the same degree of commitment as yourself and work on your bidding system. Alternatively, accept that you will probably not get much better because you don't really have the time to devote to the game. Just play because you enjoy it.

If you want to play competitive bridge locally, the English Bridge Union (Broadfields, Bicester Road, Aylesbury HP19 8AZ; tel: 01296 317 200; email: postmaster@ebu.co.uk; web: www.ebu.co.uk) or American Contract Bridge League (2990 Airways Boulevard, Memphis, TN 38116-3847; tel: 901-332 5586; email: ceo@acbl.org; web: www.acbl.org) would gladly hook you up with your local club.